Each day of this thirty-one-day devotional will challenge you to explore the Word, learn to live faithfully, and remain faithful. Get ready for a month of motivation and encouragement! I highly recommend Cynthia Heald's new book.

LINDA DILLOW, author of *Calm My Anxious Heart* and *Satisfy My Thirsty Soul*

How Cynthia can be in her eighties and yet remain relatable to me in my thirties astounds me. She teaches through story and dives into the heart of Scripture in a way that provides depth and yet ease of comprehension. As a culture, we don't honor our older generations the way we should. But as for me, I want more of what Cynthia has . . . I want to glean her great knowledge, insight, and wisdom. Why? Because she has seen Christ in a way that magnifies all.

TERESA SWANSTROM ANDERSON, Bible teacher and author of *Beautifully Interrupted*

As usual, Cynthia Heald calls me higher. She intersperses rich thoughts from her own meditation with timeless quotes from broad reading.

JEAN FLEMING, author of *Pursue the Intentional Life*

Cynthia Heald offers rock-solid wisdom embedded with gems of Scripture and quotes that will strengthen the foundation of your faith. The ten-minute readings are perfect for personal devotions or group discussions. No "fluff" on these pages—only timeless truths about what it looks like to live a faithful life before God—faithful words from a faithful woman who models what she has written and spoken about for decades.

LORRAINE PINTUS, author of *Jump Off the Hormone Swing* and coauthor of *Intimacy Ignited*

THE FAITHFUL WAY

CYNTHIA HEALD

the faithful way

REMAINING STEADFAST IN AN UNCERTAIN WORLD

NavPress

A NavPress resource published in alliance
with Tyndale House Publishers, Inc.

NavPress is the publishing ministry of The Navigators, an international
Christian organization and leader in personal spiritual development. NavPress
is committed to helping people grow spiritually and enjoy lives of meaning
and hope through personal and group resources that are biblically rooted,
culturally relevant, and highly practical.

For more information, visit www.NavPress.com.

The Faithful Way: Remaining Steadfast in an Uncertain World

Copyright © 2019 by Cynthia Heald. All rights reserved.

A NavPress resource published in alliance with Tyndale House Publishers, Inc.

Visit the author's website at www.cynthiaheald.com.

NAVPRESS and the NAVPRESS logo are registered trademarks of NavPress, The Navigators,
Colorado Springs, CO. *TYNDALE* is a registered trademark of Tyndale House Publishers, Inc.
Absence of ® in connection with marks of NavPress or other parties does not indicate an absence
of registration of those marks.

The Team: Don Pape, Publisher; Caitlyn Carlson, Acquisitions Editor; Deborah Howell, Copy
Editor; Julie Chen, Designer

Cover illustration and design by Julie Chen; copyright © Tyndale House Publishers, Inc.; all rights
reserved. Cover background texture by Lost and Taken. Author photo by Shelly Han Photography,
copyright © 2016; all rights reserved.

The Warren Wiersbe Bible Commentary: New Testament copyright © 2007 by Warren Wiersbe.
Used by permission of David C Cook. May not be further reproduced. All rights reserved.

Some of the anecdotal illustrations in this book are true to life and are included with the
permission of the persons involved. All other illustrations are composites of real situations, and
any resemblance to people living or dead is purely coincidental.

For information about special discounts for bulk purchases, please contact Tyndale House
Publishers at csresponse@tyndale.com, or call 1-800-323-9400.

ISBN 978-1-64158-025-0

Printed in China

25   24   23   22   21   20   19
7   6   5   4   3   2   1

contents

"The Father and the Child" *ix*

Introduction *xi*

DAY 1: REMAINING FAITHFUL *1*

DAY 2: GOD'S PERFECT LOVE *7*

DAY 3: GOD'S ENDURING FAITHFULNESS *13*

DAY 4: CHOOSING FAITHFULNESS *19*

DAY 5: LOVING OBEDIENCE *25*

DAY 6: LIVING WISELY *31*

DAY 7: LIVING BY FAITH *37*

DAY 8: GOD'S SUFFICIENT GRACE *43*

DAY 9: GOD'S FAITHFUL FOUNDATION *49*

DAY 10: FREE TO BE FAITHFUL *55*

DAY 11: LIVING BY THE SPIRIT *61*

DAY 12: INTENTIONAL FAITHFULNESS *67*

DAY 13: DIVINE DISCIPLINE *73*

DAY 14: TRUSTING GOD'S WILL *79*

DAY 15: UNCOMFORTABLE GRACE *85*

DAY 16: GOD'S FAITHFUL FORGIVENESS *91*

DAY 17: FACING THE CONSEQUENCES *97*

DAY 18: ACCEPTING CORRECTION *103*

DAY 19: WATCH AND PRAY *109*

DAY 20: BEING CAREFUL *115*

DAY 21: HINDRANCES TO LIVING
         THE FAITHFUL WAY *121*

DAY 22: TEMPTATION-AWARE *127*

DAY 23: FAITHFUL FELLOWSHIP *133*

DAY 24: A DISCIPLINED ATHLETE *139*

DAY 25: KEEPING IN STEP WITH THE SPIRIT *145*

DAY 26: ABIDING IN THE WORD *151*

DAY 27: FAITHFUL IN PRAYER *157*

DAY 28: THE FRUIT OF THE SPIRIT *163*

DAY 29: RUNNING FAITHFULLY *171*

DAY 30: AUTHENTIC FAITHFULNESS *177*

DAY 31: HALL OF FAITHFULNESS *183*

EPILOGUE: WELL DONE! *189*

         "The Father and the Child" *195*
         Suggestions for Group Study *197*
         Notes *199*
         About the Author *207*
         A Word about the Cover *209*

"The Father and the child"

THE CHILD SPOKE:

Father, I've been thinking about Paul's words to
Timothy: "I have fought the good fight, I have
finished the race, and I have remained faithful"
(2 Timothy 4:7).

And what are your thoughts?

I want to be faithful and run my race well, but I know
how vulnerable I am to the world's ways.

My way is the faithful way.

Yes, but it is not easy in today's world to fight the
good fight of faith.

*I am with you, giving you the strength and the power to
do what is right and to choose the way of faithfulness
in any circumstance.*

I know that I can do all things through Christ who strengthens me—and even remain faithful in an uncertain world. I guess I just need to be encouraged and reminded of your faithfulness.

Good, your heart is set to remain steadfast. I am most pleased when my children seek to live faithfully—for my best gifts are found on the faithful way.

introduction

PERHAPS IT IS FITTING that as I enter my eightieth year, I am writing a devotional study called *The Faithful Way*. The Lord has always prompted me to write on topics he knows I need, and remaining faithful in our uncertain world is an indispensable message for each of us, regardless of how old we are.

It was one of Paul's statements to Timothy that caused me to fully consider how faithfulness defines our lives. He announced, "The time of my death is near. I have fought the good fight, I have finished the race, and I have remained faithful" (2 Timothy 4:6-7). As he faced the end of his earthly days, Paul was expressing his wholehearted commitment to living as faithfully as he could for the Lord. He was not perfect, but he was passionate in wanting to live for the Christ he loved.

Paul's testimony challenges us to live in such a way that we, too, can say, "I have remained faithful." Yet living in today's culture presents countless temptations to live for ourselves and to compromise our faith. This is where we must fight the good fight and determine to remain steadfast. The consequences of choosing to live the world's way can be painful and heartbreaking. Unfaithfulness leads to unnecessary, unwelcome, and often lifetime consequences. Perhaps I have been around long enough to know that choosing to live faithfully surpasses any fleeting pleasure we might obtain by yielding to temptation. What I have discovered over the years is that God's desire for me to be faithful is an expression of his love for me. God's instruction and empowerment to live a faithful life is a gift; it is the way he created us to live.

Over the next thirty-one days, let us be intentional to choose and trust God's way. Since we are on this earth for a relatively short time, why not choose to travel the best path, where our Father guides, protects, equips, corrects, transforms, and gives our lives meaning? No other way promises the unconditional love and abundant grace of God.

The faithful way is a well-trodden path that is blessed at every turn by his presence and peace. This way leads to our eternal home, where the Lord awaits to greet us with, "Well done, my good and faithful servant" (Matthew 25:23).

I pray that you will passionately commit to choose the

faithful way and that you will finish your race with joy—because you have remained steadfast in our uncertain world.

Keep your hand in his,

Cynthia Heald

remaining faithful

I have fought the good fight, I have finished the race, and I have remained faithful.

2 TIMOTHY 4:7

Faith is the heroic effort of your life, you fling yourself in reckless confidence on God. God has ventured all in Jesus Christ to save us, now He wants us to venture our all in abandoned confidence in Him.

OSWALD CHAMBERS,
My Utmost for His Highest

ONE OF MY FAVORITE CHILDREN'S BOOKS is *Horton Hatches the Egg*, by Dr. Seuss. An irresponsible mother bird decides to go on vacation, and Horton, an elephant, faithfully sits on her nest, enduring winter storms and ridicule to keep the egg safe. Through it all he continually renews his commitment:

> *I meant what I said, and I said what I meant . . .*
> *An elephant's faithful—one hundred per cent!*[1]

In an implausible and humorous way, Dr. Seuss used Horton to express the essence of faithfulness: persevering devotedness, steadfastness, and trustworthiness. It's a priceless lesson for everyone since we all desire and highly value these qualities in our lives and relationships.

Horton's surprising reward was seeing the egg he protected produce a baby elephant bird. While such a metamorphosis is reserved for fiction, we cannot miss the parallel with the spiritual reshaping of the human heart. God delights in transforming us into new creatures. One dramatic example is the transformation of Saul from a devout Pharisee and persecutor of the early church to Paul, a passionate missionary for Christ and a New Testament author. After his blinding encounter with the Lord on the road to Damascus, Paul was commissioned as God's chosen instrument to minister and suffer for the Lord's sake. And suffer he did—yet all the while, he remained steadfast "for finishing the work assigned . . . by the Lord Jesus" (Acts 20:24).

EXPLORING THE WORD

Bible expositor A. C. Hervey wrote of Paul's faithfulness, "Through his long eventful course, in spite of all difficulties, conflicts, dangers, and temptations, he had kept the faith of Jesus Christ committed to him, inviolable, unadulterated, whole, and complete. He had not shrunk from confessing it when death stared him in the face; he had not corrupted it to meet the views of Jews or Gentiles; with courage and resolution and perseverance he had kept it to the end."[2]

In his second letter to the Corinthian church, Paul summarized his ministry experiences. Read 2 Corinthians 6:3-10 and recount some of his struggles. Record the resources he depended upon in order to remain faithful and above reproach.

LEARNING TO LIVE FAITHFULLY

Paul lived a faithful and steadfast life in the face of many trials. But we don't have to look far to discover a contrast to this kind of life. Demas was a companion of Paul during his first Roman imprisonment, but the lure of the world and the reality of Paul's second imprisonment soon overwhelmed him. We read these regrettable words in Paul's letter to

Timothy: "Timothy, please come as soon as you can. Demas has deserted me because he loves the things of this life and has gone to Thessalonica" (2 Timothy 4:9-10). Twentieth-century pastor and author Herbert Lockyer wrote of Demas,

> The prison where [Paul was] languishing seemed wretched alongside the music-haunted, scented, dazzling halls of Rome. Thus Paul had to write one of the most heartbreaking lines in his letters:
> "Demas hath forsaken me, having loved this present world."[3]

Certainly Demas was drawn to Paul's love and faith in Christ. But perhaps, despite his desire to emulate Paul's commitment to Christ, Demas had not yet wholly surrendered to live for the eternal; the temporal was still alluring. Not so with Paul. Because of God's transforming grace, Paul gratefully and purposefully rejected anything that hindered his pursuit of Christ:

> Yes, everything else is worthless when compared with the infinite value of knowing Christ Jesus my Lord. For his sake I have discarded everything else, counting it all as garbage, so that I could gain Christ.
>
> PHILIPPIANS 3:8

Faithfulness cannot be created through missionary trips or mere behavioral changes. Faithfulness begins with ardent love for the Lord and fervent determination to fling ourselves on him in reckless confidence. Paul fought the good fight of faith through hardships and calamities of every kind. Demas, apparently, was willing to abandon such a fight.

Are we seeking to fight the good fight of faith in order to remain faithful? Let us desire to fine-tune our hearts each day and become so motivated by God's grace, love, and faithfulness that we venture our all in abandoned confidence in him. Only then will we remain steadfast in an uncertain world.

REMAINING FAITHFUL

Paul's faith was tried and proven. In his letter to Timothy, he seemed to write his epitaph by proclaiming his unswerving commitment to the Lord: "I have fought the good fight, I have finished the race, and I have remained faithful" (2 Timothy 4:7).

In stillness before the Lord, ask God to search your heart while you meditate on these questions:

- How does Paul's life of faithfulness challenge you?

- When you come to the end of your race, what would you like to be able to tell others about your faithfulness?

————————————————

Father, I desire to venture my all in abandoned confidence in you. May I have the determination and confidence of Paul to fight the good fight of faith, to run my race faithfully, and to be able to say, "I have remained faithful." Amen.

————————————————

God is righteous, and he not only will not forget our work and labour of love, but he will not allow those of his servants who have devoted their powers to his cause with the greatest energy, constancy, and self-sacrifice to miss the most generous and gracious recognition at his loving hand.

W. CLARKSON, IN *The Pulpit Commentary*

God's perfect love

The LORD your God is living among you.
  He is a mighty savior.
He will take delight in you with gladness.
  With his love, he will calm all your fears.
  He will rejoice over you with joyful songs.

ZEPHANIAH 3:17

God's love for you is so infinitely intense that He
quite literally sings for joy. Such is the depth of
His affection that mere words prove paltry and
inadequate. So profoundly intimate is God's
devotion to you that He bursts forth in sacred song.

SAM STORMS, *The Singing God*

IN HIS CLASSIC BOOK *The Knowledge of the Holy*, A. W. Tozer stated, "What comes into our minds when we think about God is the most important thing about us."[4] How do our thoughts about God affect our view of and response to God? As I've contemplated what I think about God, what comes to mind immediately is the Cross. God's love in sending his Son into the world to give me eternal life is truly "past belief, past utterance, past thought."[5]

When I was in my twenties, I lived in East Asia for a year. One thing I learned is that some of the dear people in that part of the world struggle to believe in Jesus because in their minds, a "god" would not die such a shameful death. The religiously minded Jews of Jesus' day also wrestled with this idea. The Messiah they were looking for was to be a conquering king. Pastor and author Sam Storms has expounded on this point of view: "A 'crucified Messiah' was a contradiction in terms. . . . The Messiah is the embodiment of power, splendor, and triumph. Crucifixion is the embodiment of weakness, degradation, and defeat."[6]

The cross as a method of execution was used not only to kill but also to shame and dishonor. It was public for all to see. It was the ultimate humiliation—but it was also the ultimate sacrifice needed to purchase our freedom and our redemption. God demonstrated his love for us by sending his Son as a sacrifice to take away our sins (see 1 John 4:10). Now the cross is the universal symbol of his intense love that produces songs of rejoicing over us. We are profoundly and intimately loved.

God's love is the only love that is perfect, unfailing, and unconditional. A nineteenth-century scholar wrote, "The soul, until it hath found God, is ever-more seeking some love to fill it, and can find none, since the love of God Alone can content it."[7] I like the phrase *God Alone can content it*. We are equipped to walk in faithfulness when we fully embrace the magnitude of God's love and understand that his love alone can satisfy!

EXPLORING THE WORD

Author and pastor Dan Kimball wrote about the importance of understanding God's attributes: "Where our definition comes from about who 'God' is and what He is like is everything. Our morals, our ethics and our worldviews are all wrapped up in what we believe about God and how we respond to Him and His guidance. How we view ourselves is all wrapped up in what we believe about God and how He views us."[8] Any belief we have needs to be rooted in God's Word. What do the following Scriptures teach about God's love?

- Romans 8:38-39
- 1 John 4:9-10

LEARNING TO LIVE FAITHFULLY

Pastor and author Robert J. Morgan recounted this story:

> I once read of a man in Dundee, Scotland, who was confined to bed for forty years, having broken his neck in a fall at age fifteen. But his spirit remained unbroken, and his cheer and courage so inspired people that he enjoyed a constant stream of guests. One day a visitor asked him, "Doesn't Satan ever tempt you to doubt God?"
>
> "Oh, yes," replied the man. "He does try to tempt me. I lie here and see my old schoolmates driving alone in their carriages and Satan whispers, 'If God is so good, why does He keep you here all these years? Why did he permit your neck to be broken?'"
>
> "What do you do when Satan whispers these things?" asked the guest.
>
> "Ah," replied the invalid, "I take him to Calvary, show him Christ, and point to those deep wounds, and say, 'You see, he *does* love me.' And Satan has no answer to that. He flees every time."[9]

Sam Storms wrote a beautiful postscript to this story: "So the next time you are depressed and feel abandoned and are desperate for some assurance that God really loves you, fix your eyes on the 'the old rugged cross, the emblem of suffering and shame.' That is how much God loves you. Can you hear Him singing?"[10]

REMAINING FAITHFUL

Psalm 26:3 says, "Your steadfast love is before my eyes, and I walk in your faithfulness" (ESV). God's everlasting love produces a desire to be faithful to the one who sent his Son to die for us and who rejoices over us with joyful songs.

- If what we believe about God is the most important thing about us, what do you regard as true about God? How does this truth influence your commitment to remain faithful?

- As you contemplate Psalm 26:3, write down some ways you can be reminded of God's unfailing love in order to live faithfully.

- Take time to reflect on what you have studied today, and delight in his love for you.

Father, I reverently and humbly bow before you with the greatest possible gratitude for your sacrifice on the cross. It is my forever reminder of the depth of your love. May I keep your steadfast love before my eyes and walk faithfully in your faithfulness. Amen.

On a hill far away stood an old rugged cross,
The emblem of suffering and shame;
And I love that old cross, where the dearest and best
For a world of lost sinners was slain.
So I'll cherish the old rugged cross . . .
And exchange it someday for a crown.

GEORGE BENNARD, "The Old Rugged Cross"

DAY 3

God's enduring faithfulness

If we are unfaithful,
he remains faithful,
for he cannot deny who he is.

2 TIMOTHY 2:13

His faithfulness is not a demonstration of how well
you're doing; no, it's a revelation of how completely
holy, righteous, kind, and good he is. He remains
faithful even on your most unfaithful day.

PAUL DAVID TRIPP, *New Morning Mercies*

13

Whenever I read about the prophet Moses, I inevitably picture him as vintage Hollywood movie star Charlton Heston when he starred in the epic 1956 movie *The Ten Commandments*. Without question, the fascinating life of Moses and the Exodus of the Israelites from Egypt are worthy of a nearly four-hour movie!

Seeking relief from a famine, Jacob and his family traveled to Egypt and settled there. As generations passed and the number of Israelites increased, they were considered a threat and eventually were cruelly enslaved. Moses was God's choice to deliver the Israelites out of slavery.

The Lord used Moses to inflict a series of plagues upon the Egyptians with the desired result of Pharaoh's release of the Israelites. After this happened, though, Pharaoh had second thoughts and decided to pursue and recapture his slaves. With the Egyptian army close behind, the Israelites approached the Red Sea.

My favorite scene in the movie is the depiction of Moses lifting his rod, pointing it toward the Red Sea, and watching God miraculously separate the sea into great walls of water as the Israelites escape from the advancing Egyptian army. But this isn't just Hollywood magic: Scripture tells us it really happened, a breathtaking performance by a faithful God on behalf of his children (Exodus 12:31-40; 14:21).

EXPLORING THE WORD

The psalmist proclaimed, "Your unfailing love, O LORD, is as vast as the heavens; your faithfulness reaches beyond the clouds" (Psalm 36:5). Indeed, God's constancy, his trustworthiness, is expansive and boundless. What can you learn from these Scriptures about God's preeminence and steadfastness?

- Psalm 89:5-8
- Lamentations 3:22-23

LEARNING TO LIVE FAITHFULLY

Faithfulness is "adhering firmly and devotedly, as to a person, cause, or idea."[11] It is loyalty, resoluteness, and steadfastness. The Hebrew words that express God's faithfulness mean "to confirm or support," "to be certain," and "truth."[12] God, and God alone, exemplifies perfect faithfulness.

I'm inspired by the life of the British missionary Gladys Aylward, who like Moses was also a liberator. Her journey began in the 1930s when she traveled unaccompanied on a perilous journey to China to assist an older missionary. After Japan invaded China in 1937, Gladys, under great duress and hardship, led one hundred children to safety. She endured illness, malnutrition, and exhaustion, but God was with her and "parted the waters" for her and the children's safe passage.[13] Gladys's faithful life affirms the faithfulness of God—his protection, his strength, and his grace to persevere.

The apostle Paul also experienced God's strength in a most difficult time. He wrote to Timothy, "The first time I was brought before the judge, no one came with me. Everyone abandoned me. . . . But the Lord stood with me and gave me strength" (2 Timothy 4:16-17). God is our certainty, our support, and the one who never leaves us or forsakes us.

God is steadfast, and his faithfulness is not dependent on our faithfulness. We see this vividly in how Jesus responded to his disciples when the soldiers arrested Jesus, and "all his disciples deserted him and ran away" (Mark 14:50). Yet after his resurrection, Jesus appeared to the disciples (who were meeting behind locked doors!) and spoke, "Peace be with you. As the Father has sent me, so I am sending you" (John 20:21). As author Warren Wiersbe noted, "It must have given the men great joy to realize that, in spite of their many failures, their Lord was entrusting them with His Word and His work. They had forsaken Him and fled, but now He was sending them out to represent Him."[14]

Author and teacher Paul David Tripp gives us this encouragement:

> The One who created and controls the world,
> the One who is the ultimate definition of what is
> loving, true, and good, and the One who alone has

the power to finally defeat sin has chosen, because of his grace, to wrap his arms of faithful love and protection around you, and he will not let you go.

. . .

This doesn't mean that it doesn't matter how you live, but that your security is not found in your faithfulness, but in his.[15]

God's faithfulness is perfect. He faithfully delivered the Israelites through the Red Sea, and he desires to lead us faithfully as we journey. Oswald Chambers once said that "living a life of faith means never knowing where you are being led. But it does mean loving and knowing the One who is leading."[16] And truly that is the foundation of our ability to live faithfully: knowing the unfailing love and enduring faithfulness of God.

REMAINING FAITHFUL

These words from the revered hymn "Great Is Thy Faithfulness," by Thomas Chisholm, give us a beautiful picture of God's faithfulness: "Thou changest not, thy compassions they fail not; as thou hast been thou forever wilt be."[17] As God's children, we are blessed to know his great and enduring faithfulness.

- How does knowing that God wraps his faithful love and protection around you give you security?

- In what way does God's faithfulness encourage you to be faithful?

Lord, as your child, I'm most grateful that when I'm unfaithful, you continue to be faithful. May I have unwavering faith in your unchanging faithfulness. Great is your faithfulness! Amen.

Our faith corresponds with and is the answer to God's faithfulness. . . . If He is worth trusting let us trust Him. . . . Unwavering faith is the only thing that truly corresponds to unchanging faithfulness.

ALEXANDER MaCLAREN

choosing faithfulness

I have chosen the way of faithfulness;
I have set my heart on your laws.

PSALM 119:30, NIV

Let others say what they will, be it ours to say of
the Lord, "he is our refuge." But what we say we
must prove by our actions, we must fly to the Lord
for shelter, and not to an arm of flesh. The bird
flies away to the thicket, and the fox hastens to its
hole, every creature uses its refuge in the hour of
danger, and even so in all peril or fear of peril let
us flee unto Jehovah, the Eternal Protector of his
own.

CHARLES SPURGEON, *Treasury of David*

ONE OF THE MORE COMPELLING STORIES in the Bible is that of Joseph, whose father, Jacob, favored him above his other sons. As a youthful dreamer, Joseph told his brothers of the dreams he'd had about becoming the ruler over his family. His jealous brothers sold him to a passing caravan of Ishmaelite traders who took him to Egypt, where he became a trustworthy and valued manager for Potiphar, the captain of Pharaoh's guard, because "the LORD was with Joseph" (see Genesis 39:1-2).

In Potiphar's home, Joseph was in a very vulnerable position. He was young and handsome—and "Mrs." Potiphar was self-indulgent, sensual, and attracted to Joseph. Day after day, she enticed Joseph, saying, "Come and sleep with me" (see Genesis 39:7, 10).

Now, consider Joseph's circumstances: He was alone and away from home, a slave who was to serve without question, and he was subject to all the normal physical appetites of a young man. He could have easily rationalized yielding to this temptation.

Who would ever find out?

Who cares?

I can't offend her; there would be dire repercussions.

Why should I refuse?

Yet what was Joseph's response? He refused. "'Look,' he told her, 'my master trusts me with everything in his entire household. No one here has more authority than I do. He has held back nothing from me except you, because you are his wife. How could I do such a wicked thing? It would be a great sin against God'" (Genesis 39:8-9). In the midst of an extremely uncertain world, Joseph proved that choosing to be faithful is far better than trusting in our own strength to remain steadfast.

EXPLORING THE WORD

Psalm 18:2 says, "The LORD is my rock, my fortress, and my savior; my God is my rock, in whom I find protection. He is my shield, the power that saves me, and my place of safety." The Scriptures record the choices of many steadfast saints. As you read these passages, how are you encouraged to choose faithfulness?

- Joshua 24:14-15
- Daniel 3:13-18

LEARNING TO LIVE FAITHFULLY

Joseph's world parallels our current culture. There is a pervasive acceptance of the relentless pressure to pursue whatever might satisfy our desires—power, wealth, or personal gratification. Just as Joseph was enticed daily to sin, so we face continual temptation to compromise our faith. I think Joseph's faithfulness grew out of his earlier resolve to set his heart to obey God's laws.

It is extremely difficult to think clearly and choose wisely in the midst of temptation. But Joseph was intentional in his desire to remain faithful. He was able to withstand this persistent assault because at one point in his life he had apparently made a choice to be faithful. Oswald Chambers confirms this truth: "The battle is lost or won in the secret places of the will before God, never first in the external world."[18]

I like to call making this choice before God a "predecision." It is setting our hearts to choose faithfulness; it is deciding beforehand how we will respond whenever we are in a compromising or an unfavorable situation. It is choosing to be faithful as our overriding go-to option, whatever our circumstances might be.

The Good News is that we are not alone in our battle with temptation; we have a Helper, the Holy Spirit. Seventeenth-century English theologian John Owen wrote, "The Holy [Spirit] works in us and upon us, as we are fit to be wrought in and upon; that is, so as to preserve our own liberty and free obedience. . . . He works in us and with us, not against us or without us."[19]

We choose faithfulness because God is faithful. He is faithful to be the Eternal Protector of his own, who supports and sustains us when tempted. Like Joseph, our faithfulness is grounded in our trust and love for God. Undoubtedly, Joseph knew the serious consequences of his refusal (death or prison), yet he remained steadfast. He trusted God to be his rock, his refuge, and the power to save him in his hour of temptation.

God is our place of safety, but sometimes his place of safety is not what we would choose. Faithfulness does not guarantee comfort, but it does guarantee protection. We are faithful because we want to honor God and not yield to sin. This was Joseph's heart. Whether he was a slave or a prisoner or the prime minister of Egypt, he chose the way of faithfulness.

REMAINING FAITHFUL

Psalm 119:101 perfectly describes Joseph: "I have refused to walk on any evil path, so that I may remain obedient to your word." Joseph chose to be obedient and faithful to God no matter how turbulent his circumstances. May his faithfulness challenge us. In assessing your walk of faith, ponder the following questions:

- What have you learned from Joseph about choosing to be faithful?

- In order to choose faithfulness, what pre-decisions do you think you might need to make?

Father, may I choose the way of faithfulness and set my heart on your laws and ways. Thank you that you are my refuge, my place of safety, and my protector. Amen.

What a motto this is for us all! "How can I do this great wickedness?" I, for whom Christ died.

F. B. MEYER, *Joseph*

loving obedience

This is how I spend my life: obeying your
commandments.

PSALM 119:56

Love for God, then, is the only acceptable motive
for obedience to Him. This love may express itself
in a reverence for Him and a desire to please Him,
but those expressions must spring from love.

JERRY BRIDGES, *The Discipline of Grace*

THE FAITHFUL WAY cannot be separated from obedience to the God we follow. We see this truth embedded in humanity all the way back to the Garden: "The LORD God placed the man in the Garden of Eden to tend and watch over it. But the LORD God warned him, 'You may freely eat the fruit of every tree in the garden—except the tree of the knowledge of good and evil. If you eat its fruit, you are sure to die'" (Genesis 2:15-17). Here we see man's first encounter with God's authority. How would Adam and Eve respond—faithfully and obediently? Unfortunately they chose to disobey, and as a result of their choice, we, too, are confronted with the challenge of living obediently.

The Garden, humanity's first home, was indeed a paradise. Scripture tells us, "The LORD God made all sorts of trees grow up from the ground—trees that were beautiful and that produced delicious fruit" (Genesis 2:9). Adam and Eve were abundantly and beautifully provided for. They had delicious fruit. They lived freely, safely, and peacefully. The tree of the knowledge of good and evil should have held no attraction, but it was there by God's design. And so we must ask the question, Why did the Lord place this forbidden tree in the Garden?

Commentator Thomas Whitelaw helps us understand:

Virtue that stands only because it has never been assaulted is, to say the least of it, not of the highest kind. Unless man had been subjected to trial it might have remained dubious whether he obeyed of free choice or from mechanical necessity. . . . The specific commandment [that] Adam was required to observe was not severe in its terms. The limitations it prescribed were of the smallest possible description—abstinence from only one tree.[20]

Ultimately, our trust in God will determine how we respond to his commands. The way of faithfulness calls for obedience given out of love and respect to our all-wise God, who knows what is best for us.

EXPLORING THE WORD

Obedience is not a fun word! It suggests the idea of duty, submission, and not sticking up for yourself. But I appreciate this insightful observation on obedience by biblical commentator S. R. Aldridge: "Christian obedience is rendered as the joyous intelligent outcome of salvation through Christ, bringing us righteousness and life."[21] Because of Christ's gift of salvation, we should desire to follow him with gratitude and joy. What other thoughts on obedience can be discovered from the following Scriptures?

- John 14:21, 23
- 1 John 3:23-24

LEARNING TO LIVE FAITHFULLY

According to rabbinical teaching, there were more than six hundred precepts in the law of Moses. When a Pharisee approached Jesus and asked, "Teacher, which is the most important commandment in the law of Moses?" (Matthew 22:36), Jesus replied in an unexpected way, naming two commands: "'You must love the LORD your God with all your heart, all your soul, and all your mind.' . . . A second is equally important: 'Love your neighbor as yourself'" (verses 37-39).

B. C. Caffin wrote, "The love of God is the first of all the commandments. We must not be contented with our spiritual state unless we are sincerely and earnestly striving to obey it. . . . Both [commandments] say, 'Thou shalt love;' the word 'love' in both is the same . . . which is the love of reverence, respect."[22] Essentially, obedience is simply and impressively summed up by three words: *You must love.* The command to love is straightforward and foundational to our obedience.

In Psalm 119:33-35, we find this heartfelt prayer: "Teach me your decrees, O LORD; I will keep them to the end. Give me understanding and I will obey your instructions; I will put them into practice with all my heart. Make me walk along the path of your commands, for that is where my happiness is found." The psalmist's desire to obey stands in stark contrast to Adam and Eve's claim to independence from God, choosing to love their supposed freedom more than him.

In his sovereignty, God desires our freely given obedience and love rather than mechanical, robotic responses to his commands. We are God's children, and our Father is pleased when we delight to do his will: "A master may be satisfied with formal obedience, and so may a king . . . but a *father* never is. He wants his child to obey; but he never can rest content until his child *loves to obey*, and is manifestly happy in his obedience."[23]

We obey not to be loved, but because we are loved. In return we demonstrate our love to God by obeying. We obey not to be blessed, but to be a blessing to the Lord. Obedience is its own reward. As the hymn says, "It will be worth it all when we see Jesus!"[24]

REMAINING FAITHFUL

John MacArthur, pastor and author, made this distinction between a servant and slave: "Servants are *hired*; slaves are *owned*."[25] First Corinthians 6:19-20 tells us, "You do not belong to yourself, for God bought you with a high price." Paul explained to the Philippian believers that Jesus paid this price when he gave up his divine privileges and "took the humble position of a slave. . . . He humbled himself in obedience to God and died a criminal's death on a cross" (Philippians 2:7-8). We now belong to the Lord and have the privilege of serving and obeying the King of all kings and the Lord of all lords.

- How does understanding that you have been bought with a price change your perspective on what obedience should look like?

- As you consider your obedience to God, spend time in prayer asking him to fill your heart with his love so that you will love to obey.

Father, how grateful I am for Christ's selfless obedience to your will. Lord, may I follow his faithful way and be your loving, faithful, and obedient servant. Amen.

The passion of Christianity is that I deliberately sign away my own rights and become a bond-slave of Jesus Christ.

OSWALD CHAMBERS, *My Utmost for His Highest*

living wisely

Those who trust their own insight are foolish,
but anyone who walks in wisdom is safe.

PROVERBS 28:26

One of the dark delusions of sin is that it causes us
at points to buy into the insane thought that we
might be smarter than God.

PAUL DAVID TRIPP, *New Morning Mercies*

WHILE ATTENDING A PARTY, "Jake" consumed too much alcohol, yet he insisted on driving home alone. As he sped his car in a drunken stupor, he swerved into the median, causing a devastating accident that left him seriously injured. As a result, his left arm needed to be amputated.

A few years earlier, this young man had placed his faith in Christ. Jake knew the truth and wisdom of God's love and grace, but he chose to rely on his own insight and live selfishly. As he recuperated and reflected on his actions, he confessed his sin and was forgiven. Spiritually he was renewed and restored in his relationship with the Lord, but physically he suffered the consequence of his foolishness for the rest of his life. Proverbs 9:12 tells us, "If you become wise, you will be the one to benefit. If you scorn wisdom, you will be the one to suffer."

It is a profound turning point in our lives when we realize we are not smarter than God! God knows how we should live—he created us. We are his idea. Psalm 119:73 is a great verse: "You made me; you created me. Now give me the sense to follow your commands." This excellent prayer acknowledges God's sovereignty and our desire to live wisely. Thankfully, he hasn't left us to stumble through life without his book of wisdom and his personal guidance.

Author David Roper observed, "The wise are those who live well, and who, when finished, have something to show for it. They have accomplished something eternally worthwhile. . . . It's not what we *know* that makes us wise, but what we *are*."[26] In James 1:5, we are told, "If you need wisdom, ask our generous God, and he will give it to you. He will not rebuke you for asking." Seeking God's wisdom assures us of staying on the faithful way.

EXPLORING THE WORD

Loving God reverently means fearing God as our Creator, Father, and sovereign Savior King who is all-wise and worthy to be obeyed. Psalm 111:10 tells us, "Fear of the LORD is the foundation of true wisdom. All who obey his commandments will grow in wisdom."

- As you read Proverbs 2:1-11, record what you learn about acquiring wisdom.

LEARNING TO LIVE FAITHFULLY

The first boundary God gave was in the Garden of Eden, and it was, in a sense, a test in trusting God. Pastor John Piper interpreted God's warning this way:

If you eat of that one [tree] you will be saying to me, "I am smarter than you. I am more authoritative than you. I am wiser than you are. I think I can care for myself better than you care for me. You are not a very good Father. And so I am going to reject you." . . . So don't eat from the tree, because you will be rejecting me and all my good gifts and all my wisdom and all my care.[27]

This is a sobering reminder that when we trust ourselves more than we trust God, we are rejecting all that God desires and has planned for us.

Asa, king of Judah, was faced with an attack by an Ethiopian army nearly twice the size of his own. He cried out to the Lord, "O LORD, no one but you can help the powerless against the mighty! Help us, O LORD our God, for we trust in you alone" (2 Chronicles 14:11). God answered the king's prayer, and the enemy fled. Later in Asa's reign, King Baasha of Israel invaded Judah. With this challenge, however, Asa sent gold and silver from the Temple treasuries to the king of Aram, asking him for an alliance with Judah.

The prophet Hanani came to King Asa with this reproof: "Don't you remember what happened to the Ethiopians and Libyans and their vast army, with all of their chariots and charioteers? At that time you relied on the LORD, and he handed them over to you. The eyes of the LORD search the whole earth in order to strengthen those whose hearts are fully committed to him. What a fool you have been! From now on you will be at war" (2 Chronicles 16:8-9).

Asa was not smarter than God. He trusted in himself,

acted foolishly, and forfeited God's protection and safe-keeping. He suffered consequences that he could have avoided had he trusted God's way and wisdom.

REMAINING FAITHFUL

When I began to grow in Christ, some of the first verses I memorized were Proverbs 3:5-6: "Trust in the LORD with all your heart; do not depend on your own understanding. Seek his will in all you do, and he will show you which path to take." I'm grateful that this truth has been in my heart all these years, for it has continually reminded me of the foolishness of relying on my own wisdom and the blessing of trusting in God's wisdom to lead me. In reality, I don't want to miss out on anything God has planned for me. I learned a long time ago the unmistakable truth that I am not smarter than God.

As you sit quietly before the Lord, take time to reflect on the following thoughts:

- What are one or two ways you have seen or experienced the foolishness of self-reliance?

- As you think about your life, in what ways do you seek the safety of God's will and wisdom?

- Use Proverbs 2:1-11 as a basis for prayerfully communicating your desire to walk in wisdom.

Father, thank you that I can cry out for insight and ask for understanding. May your wisdom enter my heart and your knowledge fill me with joy so that I might live wisely. Amen.

You cannot trust God too much, nor trust yourself too little.

CHARLES SPURGEON,
Spurgeon's Sermons, Volume 20

living by faith

We are made right with God by placing our faith
in Jesus Christ. And this is true for everyone who
believes, no matter who we are.

ROMANS 3:22

Faith is unutterable trust in God, trust which
never dreams that He will not stand by us.

OSWALD CHAMBERS,
My Utmost for His Highest

As a young boy in Prussia, George was a thief, a liar, and a gambler. By the age of ten, he was stealing government money from his father. When he was fourteen years old, he was playing cards with friends and drinking while his mother was dying. Spending several weeks in prison marked his sixteenth year. Although he enrolled as a divinity student at the University of Halle Seminary in Germany, George described himself as a person of wicked behavior with an unrepentant spirit:

> Despite my sinful lifestyle and cold heart, God had mercy on me. I was as careless about Him as ever. I had no Bible and had not read any Scripture for years. I seldom went to church; and, out of custom only, I took the Lord's Supper twice a year. I never heard the gospel preached. Nobody told me that Jesus meant for Christians, by the help of God, to live according to the Holy Scriptures.[28]

While at the university, a fellow student, Beta, invited him to a Christian prayer meeting that radically changed George's perspective. When George reflected on that evening in his autobiography, he explained, "That evening was the turning point in my life. . . . [I] became very different."[29] He began reading the Bible regularly and discussing Christianity with others who attended. As the Holy Spirit worked in George's heart, George not only gradually changed his behavior to match his newfound faith but also hoped to become a missionary so he could share this faith with others. Faithfulness to that hope defined the rest of his life: George Müller did indeed become a missionary in his own country and is remembered for his ministry to orphans, providing them education and speaking to them about the hope of Jesus.

Müller made an all-important, life-changing choice: to leave his old way of life and begin a new way of living by faith. For each of us, traveling the faithful way begins with this same choice—first to accept by faith the Good News that Jesus died on the cross for our sins, and then to exercise that faith by choosing to lay aside our own desires and purpose and follow our gracious God wholeheartedly.

EXPLORING THE WORD

George Müller's life was altered because he was willing to receive the grace and salvation freely offered to him when he placed his faith in Christ. Warren Wiersbe explains the profound role of grace in our faith: "Grace means salvation completely apart from any merit or works on our part. Grace means that God does it all for Jesus' sake! Our salvation is the gift of God."[30] What do these Scriptures teach about grace?

- Romans 3:23-24
- Romans 8:31-34

LEARNING TO LIVE FAITHFULLY

On Palm Sunday in 1951, I began to live by faith. As a twelve-year-old I was taken down to the front of the church and asked, "Do you believe that Jesus Christ is the Son of God and that he died on the cross for your sins?" Although it was many years ago, I still remember my yes. That day, I was made right with God by placing my faith in Jesus Christ, and I began my new life of faith.

As I have grown, his presence has motivated me to fight the good fight of faith and endeavor to live faithfully. Years ago, our family took a giant step of faith and moved from Texas to Arizona to serve in a Christian ministry. We were confident of God's leading, but we had to exercise our faith to leave family and friends and move to a place where we knew no one. As we look back now, we realize that if we had not moved, we would have missed out on all God had planned for us here. I have lived long enough to know that choosing to walk by faith is the best and most blessed way to live. As the prophet Jeremiah proclaimed, "Blessed are those who trust in the LORD and have made the LORD their hope and confidence" (Jeremiah 17:7). How very, very true.

Evangelical theologian Donald G. Bloesch observed,

The deepest meaning of the cross is that God, out of his incomparable love, chose to identify himself with

our plight and affliction. The suffering of Christ
was the suffering of vicarious love, and not simply
a penal suffering canceling human debt. Salvation
means that Christ's merits are transferred to the
deficient sinner and also that God's forgiveness is
extended to the undeserving sinner. . . . [Christ]
gives sinners a writ of pardon and embraces them as
a loving shepherd who has found the lost sheep.[31]

George Müller experienced this very pardon—and entered into a life of faithfulness as a result. After placing his faith in Christ, he settled in Bristol, England, where he pastored the same church for over sixty-six years and eventually cared for more than ten thousand orphans. George Müller never directly sought donations from specific individuals but relied on the Almighty to provide what was needed.[32] Having accepted God's gracious gift of salvation, Müller chose to live by faith.

REMAINING FAITHFUL

Lawrence Richards, a Bible commentator and professor, provided this explanation of faith: "It is through faith that God gives salvation and righteousness. It is in the [New Testament] that we see with unmistakable clarity that faith is a personal response to God and a complete commitment of ourselves to him. There also we see that faith calls for a continuing relationship of response to Jesus' word."[33] When we have received

Christ for salvation, pardon, and peace, then humbly and gratefully we should desire to walk the way of faithfulness.

- What is your faith story of receiving Christ as your Savior and Lord? (If you are unsure, take time now to pray over Romans 3:23-24 and Romans 6:23.)

- How has the way you live your daily life been altered in response to God's kindness, mercy, and love?

- Prayerfully express your gratitude for the free gift of God's salvation and for the adventure of living by faith.

Dear Lord, thank you for your grace and forgiveness on my behalf that has given me a brand-new way to live. May I live faithfully in joyful response to your extravagant grace. Amen.

Faith so completely takes God at his word that it is willing to do what he says and stay inside his boundaries. Faith is a response of your heart to God that completely alters the way you live your life. You don't just think by faith; you live by faith.

PAUL DAVID TRIPP, *New Morning Mercies*

God's sufficient grace

He said to me, "My grace is sufficient for you, for
my power is made perfect in weakness."

2 CORINTHIANS 12:9, ESV

To live by grace means we understand that God's
blessing on our lives is not conditioned by our
obedience or disobedience but by the perfect
obedience of Christ. It means that out of a grateful
response to the grace of God, we seek to understand
His will and to obey Him, not to be blessed, but
because we have been blessed.

JERRY BRIDGES, *Transforming Grace*

AFTER RETURNING HOME from the grocery store and putting away the food, I went to get something out of my purse— but I couldn't find it. Alarmed, I mentally retraced my steps and realized that in my haste, I probably had left my purse in the grocery cart. I jumped in the car and hurried back to the store. I was heartsick that I could be so preoccupied and leave my valuables in a basket in a public parking lot. I began to think about everything that would need to be canceled, renewed, and replaced—a lengthy and tedious process I dreaded. As I entered the store and headed to the manager's office, I saw a dear man holding up my purse for me to see. Apparently he could tell by the stricken look on my face why I was there. I had to restrain myself from giving him a big hug. I learned that a very honest soul had brought it in for safekeeping.

I tell this story, as inconsequential as it is, because it illustrates an aspect of God's grace: his undeserved kindness. In reality, I didn't deserve to get my purse back. I was solely responsible for not being more attentive and careful. But since I did get it back, I considered this an unmerited blessing that was not dependent on what I did or did not do. At the same time, I also knew that if I had to deal with all the missing cards and other essentials, I could do it, because God's grace is not only sufficient in itself but also gives strength to accomplish what needs to be done.

So God's grace is twofold: His grace, or unmerited favor,

is bestowed upon us when we accept Christ's sacrifice for our sins—this is his grace *for* us. His grace is also expressed by the indwelling of the Holy Spirit, who strengthens and empowers us—this is his grace *in* us. His sufficient grace both saves and strengthens as we walk the faithful way.

EXPLORING THE WORD

Lawrence Richards stated, "Grace declares that God is merciful and loving and that he is able to act to meet our deepest need. Grace teaches that God has acted in Jesus to bring us forgiveness and new life through his atoning sacrifice on Calvary."[34] Record your thoughts as you study these Scriptures on grace:

- Romans 5:20-21
- Ephesians 2:4-9

LEARNING TO BE FAITHFUL

Scripture's first description of the apostle Paul, then called Saul, is bleak: "[He] was uttering threats with every breath and was eager to kill the Lord's followers" (Acts 9:1). Saul was passionate and persistent in this mission—until the Lord confronted him. Evangelical pastor and author Charles Swindoll summed up the life of the apostle Paul this way: "From a past of Pharisaic pride, cruel brutality, and religious unbelief, he was changed from a zealous persecutor of the church to a humble servant of Christ. And what was the reason? The grace of God."[35] In his own words, Paul related his encounter with God's saving grace: "God had mercy on me so that Christ Jesus could use me as a prime example of his great patience with even the worst sinners. Then others will realize that they, too, can believe in him and receive eternal life" (1 Timothy 1:16). Paul experienced God's grace *for* him, and then he spent his life comprehending God's grace *in* him.

Just as Paul was relentless in his pursuit of Christians, God is relentless in his pursuit of producing Christlike character in his children. For Paul, this meant a "thorn" in his flesh sent to keep him from becoming proud. Three times Paul prayed for the thorn to be removed, and each time the Lord answered, "My grace is all you need. My power works best in weakness." And Paul's response was, "So now I am glad to boast about my weaknesses, so that the power of Christ can work through me" (see 2 Corinthians 12:5-9). Swindoll observed, "It was grace that made him 'content with weaknesses.' Once that contentment came, strength revived within him. Not even insults, distresses, or persecutions could sideline the apostle once grace gave him contentment in weakness."[36]

Paul considered himself to be the worst of sinners (see 1 Timothy 1:15), and he more than anyone fully understood

God's extravagant grace, freely given at great cost through the blood of Christ. In grateful response Paul sought to live faithfully as an obedient servant. Like all of us who follow Jesus, he received a rich blessing of sufficient grace and love he knew he did not deserve.

REMAINING FAITHFUL

Paul was assured that God's grace was sufficient for all his needs, and he knew that God's grace alone was sufficient for his salvation. Because of God's kindness, he fought the good fight, ran his race, and remained faithful to the Lord, compelled by the love and grace of Christ. Thoughtfully respond to these questions as you consider the grace you have received:

- A "thorn" can be anything you have no control over but must live with and endure. In light of this definition, how have you experienced the sufficiency of God's grace? If you have not, what steps can you take to receive God's sufficient grace for your thorn?

- Express your desire to rely on and be content with God's grace, whatever your need may be.

Father, how grateful I am for the surpassing riches of your grace, which is all-sufficient **for** *me and* **in** *me. I pray that the overwhelming nature of your love and grace will bring about contentment in my weaknesses. Amen.*

God's grace does not fail, but we can fail to depend on God's grace.

WARREN WIERSBE,
The Wiersbe Bible Commentary: New Testament

God's faithful foundation

God declared an end to sin's control over us by
giving his Son as a sacrifice for our sins. He did this
so that the just requirement of the law would be
fully satisfied for us, who no longer follow our sinful
nature but instead follow the Spirit.

ROMANS 8:3-4

My hope lives not because I am not a sinner, but
because I am a sinner for whom Christ died; my
trust is not that I am holy, but that being unholy,
He *is* my righteousness. My faith rests not upon
what I am or shall be or feel or know, but in what
Christ is, in what He has done, and in what He is
now doing for me. Hallelujah!

CHARLES SPURGEON, *Morning and Evening*

As we seek to live the faithful way, it is helpful to understand what *regeneration*, *justification*, and *sanctification* mean for our life and faith. *Regeneration* is simply new birth, a new beginning. Jesus told Nicodemus, "I tell you the truth, unless you are born again, you cannot see the Kingdom of God" (John 3:3). When we accept Christ as our personal Savior, we are born again—regenerated.

William Evans, a teacher of biblical interpretation and an author, explained *justification* this way:

> It is a change in a man's relation or standing before God. . . . It is a change from guilt and condemnation to acquittal and acceptance. Regeneration has to do with the change of the believer's nature; justification, with the change of his standing before God. . . . To justify means to set forth as righteous; to declare righteous in a legal sense; to put a person in a right relation. It does not deal, at least not directly, with character or conduct.[37]

Paul emphasized these characteristics of justification in Romans 3:24: "God, in his grace, freely makes us right in his sight. He did this through Christ Jesus when he freed us from the penalty for our sins." Grasping the enormous significance of regeneration and justification has encouraged me to live faithfully. Confidence in my regeneration and assurance of my justification especially help me when I am unfaithful. I remember that I have been freed from the power of sin and am now accepted as God's child, and that I need only seek my Father's forgiveness to be restored. Justification gives me freedom, peace, and security, and in grateful response I desire to be faithful. Romans 8:1-2 shows us the extraordinary gift we have been given:

> There is no condemnation for those who belong to Christ Jesus. And because you belong to him, the power of the life-giving Spirit has freed you from the power of sin that leads to death.

Martyn Lloyd-Jones, the pastor at London's Westminster Chapel for nearly thirty years in the 1900s, defined *sanctification* this way:

> That gracious and continuous operation of the Holy Spirit by which He delivers the justified sinner from the pollution of sin, renews his whole nature in the image of God, and enables him to perform good works. . . . So sanctification is really God's way of dealing with the problem of sin after our regeneration and justification.[38]

Awareness of God's sanctifying work gives me a sense of his protection and involvement in my life as I seek to live faithfully. I am not just regenerated and justified. God continues his work by the indwelling Holy Spirit, whose purpose is to conform me to the image of Christ as I live faithfully.

DIFFERENCES BETWEEN JUSTIFICATION AND SANCTIFICATION	
Justification	**Sanctification**
Legal standing	Internal condition
Once for all time	Continuous throughout life
Entirely God's work	We cooperate
Perfect in this life	Not perfect in this life
The same in all Christians	Greater in some than in others[39]

EXPLORING THE WORD

Regeneration initiates a definite moral change: We are born again. Justification is a once-and-for-all act and takes place outside us, while sanctification is a continual process and takes place within us. How do these verses further your understanding of justification and sanctification?

- Romans 3:21-24; Titus 3:4-7
- 2 Thessalonians 2:13-16

LEARNING TO LIVE FAITHFULLY

Since 1951, I have been confident in my regeneration. Understanding God's work of justification and sanctification assures me of my standing before God and of his continuing sanctifying work in my life.

I'm forever grateful for Christ's sacrifice on the cross on my behalf. Christ, who never sinned, experienced sin in its vilest and fullest form so that I could be freed from the power of sin and made right with God. It is by God's undeserved grace, and his alone, that I am restored to right standing before him. Ephesians 2:8 says, "God saved you by his grace when you believed. And you can't take credit for this; it is a gift from God." This is Good News, and I need to preach this gospel to myself daily in order to remember God's great love and rich mercy.

Recalling God's faithfulness motivates me to live faithfully by submitting to the Holy Spirit's guidance and sanctifying work. Samuel D. Gordon, an early-twentieth-century author and lay minister, admonished, "As surely as men are now urged to accept Jesus as the great step in life, so surely should they be instructed to yield themselves to the Holy Spirit's control that Jesus' plan for their lives may be carried through."[40]

Because God's costly, sacrificial love purchased my freedom, I want Jesus' plan for my life. I want to serve my faithful God, who is completely holy, righteous, kind, and good. I want to fight the good fight, I want to run my race, and I want to remain faithful.

REMAINING FAITHFUL

The Romans passage at the beginning of today's reading ends by saying that we are those "who no longer follow our sinful nature but instead follow the Spirit" (8:4). The result of justification and regeneration is that I'm no longer obligated to follow my sinful nature; the result of sanctification is that I follow the Spirit. Knowing this gives me a sense of his care and involvement as I seek to live faithfully.

- How can the explanations of justification and sanctification encourage your desire and willingness to live a faithful life?

Father, thank you for the remarkable sacrifice of your Son on my behalf. Now I am a new creation and have the blessing of submitting to and following the Spirit. Truly such amazing love does demand "my soul, my life, my all." Amen.

When I survey the wondrous cross, on which the Prince of glory died,
My richest gain I count but loss, and pour contempt on all my pride. . . .
Were the whole realm of nature mine, that were a present far too small;
Love so amazing, so divine, demands my soul, my life, my all.

ISAAC WATTS,
"When I Survey the Wondrous Cross"

free to be faithful

*We know that our old sinful selves were crucified with
Christ so that sin might lose its power in our lives.
We are no longer slaves to sin. For when we died with
Christ we were set free from the power of sin.*

ROMANS 6:6-7

*Christ rules by the golden sceptre of grace, and
he will not let sin have dominion over those that
are willing subjects to that rule. . . . Grace which
accepts the willing mind, which is not extreme
to mark what we do amiss, which leaves room
for repentance, which promises pardon upon
repentance; and what can be to an ingenuous mind
a stronger motive than this to have nothing to do
with sin? Shall we sin against so much goodness,
abuse such love?*

MATTHEW HENRY,
Commentary on the Whole Bible, Volume 6

WHEN WE ACCEPT Christ's sacrifice on the cross, our relationship to sin completely changes. Sin is no longer our master, no longer in control of our lives. We are free to be faithful. But we live in a corrupt world, constantly surrounded by advertised enticements to sin. It is not easy "to have nothing to do with sin" in today's culture.

But by the grace of God, we can live faithful lives in the midst of the sin around us. Retired NBA player A. C. Green has lived in such a way. After graduating from high school, he attended a church service where he accepted Christ. He was a star basketball player at Oregon State and became part of a Bible study and grew in his faith. The Los Angeles Lakers drafted him in the first round. In his second game he scored seventeen points and made sixteen rebounds; he was the first Laker rookie in more than two decades to play in every game. Even though surrounded by the pressures of a life in professional sports, A. C. remained firm in his faith. He vowed to remain pure before marriage, and other players teased and tempted him because of that commitment. But despite his young age, he did not allow his teammates to influence his lifestyle. He was faithful to his word, and he married at age thirty-eight.[41] Because A. C. had been set free from the power of sin, he was free to be faithful.

EXPLORING THE WORD

In Christ, we are free from the power of sin—free to be faithful. Lawrence O. Richards wrote, "Only when you and I willingly submit to the lordship of Jesus Christ can we learn what freedom truly is."[42] Grace does free us, but we must willingly submit to the grace that delivers us from sin's control. How do these verses help you understand your freedom from sin?

- Romans 6:12-14
- Galatians 2:20

LEARNING TO LIVE FAITHFULLY

Christ's sacrifice on our behalf sets us free from sin in two ways: substitution and identification. Warren Wiersbe composed a chart clarifying these two powerful truths:

Romans 3:21–5:21	Romans 6–8
Substitution: He died for me	Identification: I died with Him
He died *for* my sins	He died *unto* sin
He paid sin's penalty	He broke sin's power

Wiersbe further explained, "Sin is a terrible master, and it finds a willing servant in the human body. The body is not sinful; the body is neutral. It can be controlled either by sin or by God. But man's fallen nature, which is not changed at conversion, gives sin a beachhead from which it can attack and then control. . . . God does not command us to become dead to sin. He tells us that we *are* dead to sin and alive unto God, and then commands us to act on it."[43]

Understanding our freedom from sin is crucial to knowing that we are not bound by sin. We can no longer say, "The devil made me do it." The penalty for our sin has been paid and the power of sin broken, but acting on this truth takes effort—it takes making intentional choices.

One struggle I have is allowing sin to control my tongue. A verse that dwells deeply in my heart is, "Let no unwholesome word proceed from your mouth, but only such a word as is good for edification according to the need of the moment, so that it will give grace to those who hear" (Ephesians 4:29, NASB). I want my speech to be kind and gracious, but often I end up speaking too quickly and carelessly. Embracing the facts that sin has lost its power in my life and that I have the indwelling Holy Spirit to keep me from yielding to sin is monumental. Because I'm still in the process of learning to control my tongue, I'm thankful for God's grace, which includes repentance and restoration. Most important, though, I am thankful that God's grace includes freedom from sin's control.

Matthew Henry, a Puritan minister and Bible expositor, spoke beautifully of God's "golden sceptre of grace." God does not make us obey him. He lives in us and leads us, but we must be willing subjects to his rule. Because of the cross, we now have a choice to live faithfully. As Henry said, "Shall we sin against so much goodness, abuse such love?"[44]

REMAINING FAITHFUL

Living in the freedom of God's grace doesn't mean that we are free to do what we please. Rather, it means we are free to do what pleases the Lord. Countless people are under the impression they are free because they can choose to enjoy and participate in whatever the world has to offer. David Roper noted, "Freedom is not the power to do what we want. (That's the worst sort of slavery.) It is the power to do what we should—to be godlike in all we do and say."[45]

- In what area of your life do you struggle with letting sin have control? Prayerfully consider what you sense the Lord telling you to do.

- What would daily submission to the rule of Christ's grace look like for you?

———

Father, how very grateful I am that you have freed me from the power of sin. I humbly admit my need of your grace, and I humbly submit to your rule. Thank you for your goodness and love, and thank you for the privilege of living faithfully for you. Amen.

———

Let us, then, renounce the reign of sin, and accept the reign of grace.

R. M. EDGAR, IN *The Pulpit Commentary*

living by the Spirit

God has given us his Spirit as proof that we live in
him and he in us.

1 JOHN 4:13

Jesus died on the cross to make freedom from sin
possible. *The Holy Spirit dwells within me to*
make freedom from sin actual. *The Holy Spirit*
does in *me what Jesus did* for *me.*

S. D. GORDON, *Quiet Talks on Power*

GOD DOES NOT LEAVE US ON OUR OWN to pursue this faithful way. No, he lives within us and equips us through the Holy Spirit.

When I reflect on the Holy Spirit's work, a story about D. L. Moody comes to mind:

> When a group of British pastors was discussing the advisability of inviting evangelist D. L. Moody to their city for a crusade, one man asked, "Why must it be Moody? Does D. L. Moody have a monopoly on the Holy Spirit?" Quietly one of the other pastors replied, "No, but it's evident that the Holy Spirit has a monopoly on D. L. Moody."[46]

What a gift! The Spirit of God dwells within, equipping us with everything we need to follow him faithfully. Here are a few reasons why we want the Holy Spirit to have a monopoly on our lives:

- We have *confidence in our adoption*: "All who are led by the Spirit of God are children of God" (Romans 8:14).

- The Holy Spirit *empowers us to deny the desires of the flesh*: "Let the Holy Spirit guide your lives. Then you won't be doing what your sinful nature craves" (Galatians 5:16).

- The Spirit *teaches us all things*: "The Spirit teaches you everything you need to know, and what he teaches is true—it is not a lie" (1 John 2:27).

- We are assured that when we live in the Spirit, we *bear his fruit*: "love, joy, peace, patience, kindness, goodness, faithfulness, gentleness, and self-control" (Galatians 5:22-23).

- The Holy Spirit *intercedes for us*: "The Holy Spirit prays for us with groanings that cannot be expressed in words. And the Father who knows all hearts knows what the Spirit is saying, for the Spirit pleads for us believers in harmony with God's own will" (Romans 8:26-27).

- The Holy Spirit bestows his *gifts*: "There are different kinds of spiritual gifts, but the same Spirit is the source of them all" (1 Corinthians 12:4).

- The Holy Spirit *strengthens* us: "I pray that from his glorious, unlimited resources he will empower you with inner strength through his Spirit" (Ephesians 3:16).

EXPLORING THE WORD

The ministry of the Holy Spirit is multifaceted. He is our all-sufficient guide who leads from within. What additional insights concerning the Holy Spirit can you find in these Scriptures?

- John 14:16-17
- 2 Corinthians 3:16-18

LEARNING TO LIVE FAITHFULLY

I like pastor John Piper's picture of what it looks like to follow the Spirit's leading: "The Spirit is not a leader like the pace car in the 'Daytona 500.' He is a leader like a locomotive on a train. We do not follow in our strength. We are led by *his* power. So 'walk by the Spirit' means stay hooked up to the divine source of power and go wherever he leads. . . . *Our* wills are deeply involved. We must want to be coupled to the locomotive."[47]

At the heart of following the Spirit's leading is the reality that we are not leading. We must choose to take the "train car" of our life and permanently connect it to the "engine" of the Spirit. We are on his track, trusting in the journey he has planned for us. We are no longer in control. The Holy Spirit now guides us, and we are freed from carrying out the desires of our flesh.

The apostle Paul described how he lived this way: "I have been crucified with Christ. It is no longer I who live, but Christ who lives in me. And the life I now live in the flesh I live by faith in the Son of God, who loved me and gave himself for me" (Galatians 2:20, ESV). Paul gladly exchanged his life for Christ's life because of Jesus' love and sacrifice on the cross. Expositor F. W. Adeney commented, "Saint Paul feels that he has so given himself up to Christ that the ruling power in him is no longer self but Christ. This is true Christianity. It is life. We die that we may live."[48]

I know the reality of dying in order to truly live. When I was twenty-six years old, I didn't know about the train analogy, but I had been challenged with the analogy of myself as a car driving down the highway of life. I had invited Jesus into my "car," but I was in the driver's seat. In July 1965 I sensed the Lord prompting me to give him the steering wheel of my life. I knew he was asking me to relinquish control so that he could drive and lead me on the path he had for me. That was a very special and significant day because it was the day I "died" to myself and began to truly live.

A. W. Tozer gave us this somber reminder: "Though every believer has the Holy Spirit, the Holy Spirit does not have every believer."[49] We need to be sure we are yielding to the Spirit's control. If you desire to live the faithful way, couple yourself to his divine power, turn over the steering wheel of your life, and live in the power and freedom that only the Spirit can give. Let him monopolize your life!

REMAINING FAITHFUL

Galatians 2:20 has always been one of my favorite verses. It continually reminds me of the Lord's loving presence in my life and of his ministry in leading and empowering me to live faithfully.

- In what way have you surrendered your will to the control of the Holy Spirit?

- What hindrances might keep the Holy Spirit from having a monopoly in your life?

———————————

Father, how can I express my thanks for the privilege of being your child and for the empowering ministry of your Spirit in my life? May I willingly follow and live by the Spirit. Amen.

———————————

The Spirit bears the character of Christ and impresses that character on those who submit to it.

JAMES D. G. DUNN, IN *The Portable Seminary*

intentional faithfulness

You have charged us
  to keep your commandments carefully.
Oh, that my actions would consistently
  reflect your decrees!

PSALM 119:4-5

So that sin is always acting, always conceiving,
always seducing and tempting. . . . The saints,
whose souls breathe after deliverance from its
perplexing rebellion, know there is no safety
against it but in a constant warfare.

JOHN OWEN,

Of the Mortification of Sin in Believers

IN FRONT OF A GAS STATION in Johannesburg, South Africa, sits a chalkboard that offers an insightful daily quote to passersby. Some people even drive out of their way to read the new selection for the day! The truth of one of the quotations made me smile and also made me think: "Don't do something permanently stupid because you're temporarily upset."[50] Perhaps a more biblical spin on this quotation might read, "Don't do something permanently foolish because you are temporarily tempted."

Probably no one could testify to the accuracy of that statement more than the renowned prophet Moses. Called by God to deliver the Israelites from slavery in Egypt, Moses had the additional responsibility of leading the Israelites to Canaan, the Promised Land. Twice during this journey, Moses was called to provide water for the people. The first occurrence was at Mount Sinai, where God instructed Moses to "strike the rock" (Exodus 17:6) to bring forth water. He obeyed, and there was water for everyone. The second time was when they camped at Kadesh in the wilderness of Zin. The congregation gathered to complain and reproach Moses and Aaron for not providing for their needs, especially water.

To supply water this time, God commanded Moses to "speak" to the rock that stood before the people. But a temporarily irritated and angry Moses disregarded God's directive, and instead of speaking to the rock, he "struck" the rock. Water gushed forth, but God was not pleased. The Scriptures tell us of God's displeasure: "The LORD said to Moses and Aaron, 'Because you did not trust me enough to demonstrate my holiness to the people of Israel, you will not lead them into the land I am giving them!'" (Numbers 20:12).

Moses was still loved by God, and he did get to *see* Canaan, but he suffered an unnecessary consequence: He was not able to fulfill his lifelong mission of delivering the Israelites into the Promised Land. Moses did something permanently foolish because he was temporarily tempted.

EXPLORING THE WORD

Unfaithfulness can have its consequences. In moments of temptation and self-service, we have the potential of choosing foolishness; but in our epigraph for today, John Owen reminds us that our safety is in maintaining a constant awareness that we are in a battle. Study these verses for encouragement to remain steadfast:

- Psalm 119:80
- 2 Thessalonians 1:11-12

LEARNING TO LIVE FAITHFULLY

Moses was a man who loved, served, and walked intimately with God. He was a great man of faith, beloved by God and known as God's friend to the extent that when he died, the

Lord buried him. As Herbert Lockyer noted, Moses was "the only man in the Bible to have God as his undertaker (Deut. 34:6)."[51]

Yet Moses was just as human as we are and was provoked to unrighteous anger that dishonored God. Certainly God forgave him, but Moses paid a price for a moment of disobedience. American Bible scholar Charles Ryrie observed, "Here is a warning to us that forgiveness of sin does not always carry with it alleviation of the consequences of that sin."[52]

We can be confident in God's love for us, but we must comprehend that part of his love is expressed though consequences for disobedience. Since this is true, why not choose to be faithful and forgo consequences that God never intended for us to have? However, we should not choose to be faithful solely to avoid discipline. Our faithfulness must originate from grateful hearts for God's unfailing love and mercy toward us. He is a faithful God who is more than worthy of our faithfulness.

Paul David Tripp wrote of God's faithfulness, "He is able and willing to meet you in your moments of need, even when that need is self-inflicted. . . . He will never use your weakness against you. He has no favorites and shows no partiality. . . . He is just as faithful to all of his promises on your very worst day as he is on your very best day. . . . He knows how weak and fickle your heart is, yet he continues to move toward you with unrelenting and empowering grace."[53]

After meditating on Moses' experience, I realized that we cannot presume on our past walk with God. Faithfulness in the past does not guarantee faithfulness for the future. I believe that one way to live faithfully is to practice intentionality. Before making a choice, we must be purposeful in considering God's way so that our actions reflect his decrees. We must be vigilant, deliberate, and constant in our battle to be faithful; we must be intentional to walk the faithful way.

REMAINING FAITHFUL

Understanding the significant impact of unfaithfulness is imperative as we journey toward the Promised Land. Like Moses, we are all susceptible to temptations and ungodly responses that can result in disappointing and unwanted repercussions. Prayerfully consider these questions:

- What is one way you can "be on guard" against doing something permanently foolish?

- Compose a prayer communicating your desire to be intentionally faithful.

Father, teach me how to be intentional and careful as I choose to live faithfully and wisely. Thank you for your unrelenting and empowering grace. Amen.

Whenever we fail—and fail we will, the Spirit of God will work on us and bring us to the foot of the cross where Jesus carried our failures. . . . One who draws on God's Mercy and Grace is quick to repent, but also slow to sin.

MUTUA MAHIAINI, IN *The Discipline of Grace*

divine discipline

The LORD corrects those he loves,
   just as a father corrects a child in whom he
   delights.

PROVERBS 3:12

*What is it to receive Christ? Evidently to deliver
ourselves over to his rule and authority.*

D. YOUNG, IN *The Pulpit Commentary*

MANY YEARS AGO, when I was about six years old, I was playing outside my house with my neighborhood friends, and we decided to move to another yard. I left without telling my parents. When my mom and dad didn't see me in our yard, they immediately began calling my name. Upon finding me, my father quickly ushered me to my room for a stern lecture on not leaving without their permission. To help me remember his instruction, I had to stay inside for a period of time. The message was clear: He cared about what I was doing, and I was under his protection and authority.

These same conditions apply to our relationship with God. The incredible blessing of believing in his name is that we become his children and he becomes our Father, who assumes full responsibility for our welfare. We enter a whole new world where we are "reborn—not with a physical birth resulting from human passion or plan, but a birth that comes from God" (John 1:13). We have a heavenly Father who loves us with unfailing love, and he is committed to exercising the full responsibilities of a protective father—including discipline to help us back to the faithful way.

EXPLORING THE WORD

W. Clarkson encourages us with these words concerning God's discipline: "Certainly he is seeking our truest welfare, our highest good, our lasting joy. Let each afflicted heart

ask—What is the lesson the Father wishes me to learn?"[54]
What can you learn about God's discipline from these verses?

- Hebrews 12:5-11
- Revelation 3:19

LEARNING TO LIVE FAITHFULLY

Miriam was a prophet in a very prestigious family; she was
the sister of Moses and Aaron. When an Egyptian princess
found the baby Moses in the Nile River, Miriam was there to
suggest their mother, Jochebed, as a nursemaid (see Exodus
2:1-9; 6:20). Subsequently, after the Israelites successfully
crossed the Red Sea, Miriam was at the forefront, leading the
women in praise, proclaiming the power and faithfulness of
God (Exodus 15:20).

In her later years, however, she apparently became jealous of Moses' acclaim. She convinced Aaron to join her in
challenging the leadership of Moses. The book of Numbers
recounts this painful public incident: "While they were at
Hazeroth, Miriam and Aaron criticized Moses because he
had married a Cushite woman. They said, 'Has the LORD
spoken only through Moses? Hasn't he spoken through us,
too?'" The Lord heard their complaint and descended in a
pillar of cloud at the entrance to the Tabernacle. God was
very angry, and he reprimanded Miriam and Aaron, saying,

"Of all my house, [Moses] is the one I trust. . . . So why were you not afraid to criticize my servant?" When the cloud departed, Miriam's skin was white as snow from leprosy. God's discipline was swift and noteworthy to the one who instigated this rebellion. She received a severe lecture, and her "time-out" was to stay outside the camp for seven days. After this week of discipline, she was healed and accepted back into the community (see Numbers 12:1-14).

Herbert Lockyer commented, "Miriam's greatest offense was her sarcastic rejection of the leadership of Moses. . . . [Her] chief error consisted in her effort to break down the God-given authority of Moses, and thereby imperil the unity and hope of the nation."[55] At the Red Sea, Miriam sang what could be called the national anthem of her nation, but in her latter years she became a leader of discord and division. Miriam not only questioned the leadership of Moses but also God's authority in appointing Moses as overseer. And as D. Young reminded us at the beginning of the chapter, when we are God's children, we "deliver ourselves over to his rule and authority." If we are under God's leadership, then we are subject to his correction because he desires that his children grow in Christlikeness and faithfulness.

Matthew Henry made this observation about God's discipline:

It is to correct and cure those sinful disorders which make us unlike to God, and to improve and increase those graces which are the image of God in us, that we may be and act more like our heavenly Father. God loves his children so that he would have them to be as like himself as can be, and for this end he chastises them when they need it.[56]

It is as our Good Shepherd that he corrects and increases our graces when we follow him on the faithful path. He accomplishes his purposes by using his rod and staff to protect, reprove, and comfort us. He is always seeking our truest welfare, our highest good, and our lasting joy.

REMAINING FAITHFUL

Hebrews 12:10 tells us that "God's discipline is always good for us, so that we might share in his holiness." God loves us too much to let us disobey without some correction or consequence. His delight in us impels his discipline so that we can be made "more holy, more dead to sin and the world, and more alive to God."[57]

It is imperative to acknowledge that God's love and discipline are inextricably bound together. Because God loved Miriam, he corrected her. As her faithful Father, he disciplined her to keep her on the faithful way. He does the same for us.

- As God's child, in what ways are you aware of his chastening?

- Understanding what God intends for you is essential. How would you define God's primary purpose in his discipline?

———————

Father, thank you for seeking my truest welfare through your correction. Help me to remember that because I am your beloved child, your purpose is to produce in me Christlike character and a strong family resemblance to you as my heavenly Father. Amen.

———————

In the mundane moments of our daily lives, we buy into the fallacy that we can step over God's loving and wise moral boundaries without consequences.

PAUL DAVID TRIPP, *New Morning Mercies*

trusting God's will

Those who trust in the LORD are as secure as
   Mount Zion;
      they will not be defeated but will endure forever.

PSALM 125:1

The will of God is the expression of the love of God
for His people, for His plans come from His heart.
. . . Those who rebel against God's will are denying
His wisdom, questioning His love, and tempting
the Lord to discipline them.

WARREN WIERSBE, *Be Counted*

EVERY TIME I READ the biblical account of the Israelites' refusal to enter the Promised Land after hearing about how well protected it was, I shudder—for I know the price they will pay for their lack of trust in God's plan. From the very beginning, God's purpose was for his people to live in the land of "milk and honey" (Exodus 3:8)—Canaan. God made this clear in his covenant with Abraham: "I am giving all this land, as far as you can see, to you and your descendants as a permanent possession" (Genesis 13:15).

When God sent Moses to free the Israelites from their captivity in Egypt, these were his instructions: "Say to the people of Israel: 'I am the LORD. I will free you from your oppression and will rescue you from your slavery in Egypt. . . . I will bring you into the land I swore to give to Abraham, Isaac, and Jacob. I will give it to you as your very own possession. I am the LORD!'" (Exodus 6:6-8). At Mount Sinai, God reiterated his promise concerning Canaan: "I will send my terror ahead of you and create panic among all the people whose lands you invade. I will make all your enemies turn and run" (Exodus 23:27).

God made it very clear to the Israelites that occupying Canaan was his special gift, and one that was guaranteed. Yet after sending spies to explore the land, the majority returned with this report: "We can't go up against them! They are stronger than we are!" (Numbers 13:31). Although two of the spies, Caleb and Joshua, tried to encourage the people to go immediately and conquer the land, the distrustful and resistant Israelites began weeping and rose in protest against Moses, Aaron, Joshua, and Caleb. The end result was God's sentence on his rebellious children: "You must wander in the wilderness for forty years. . . . I will certainly do these things to every member of the community who has conspired against me. They will be destroyed here in this wilderness, and here they will die!" (Numbers 14:34-35). Trusting God even when it doesn't make sense demonstrates our faith and allows us to experience the blessing of fulfilling his purposes.

EXPLORING THE WORD

Even though God had continually reassured Israel that he would go before them and make their enemies "turn and run," the Israelites placed their confidence in the judgment of men rather than in the power and promises of God. What assurances of God's protection and faithfulness do we find in these verses?

- Exodus 23:20-23
- Deuteronomy 1:26-33

LEARNING TO LIVE FAITHFULLY

True to his promise, God had brought his people to the threshold of Canaan to camp in Kadesh-Barnea. But as biblical commentator R. Winterbotham observed, "They could not enter unless their will united itself to his will, unless they chose to go on in his name and strength. Their future was at that hour in their own hands, and they wrecked it because they did not trust God, because their faith was too weak to pass into obedience in the face of serious discouragement."[58]

Caleb and Joshua heard the harmful report from the other spies with trepidation, and they told the community, "Do not rebel against the LORD, and don't be afraid of the people of the land. They are only helpless prey to us! They have no protection, but the LORD is with us! Don't be afraid of them!" (see Numbers 14:6, 9). Despite being in the minority, Caleb and Joshua spoke powerful words of faith.

Because the Israelites depended on their own understanding and did not trust God when he showed them the path to take, the result was God's judgment: "Of all those I rescued from Egypt, no one who is twenty years old or older will ever see the land . . . for they have not obeyed me wholeheartedly. The only exceptions are Caleb son of Jephunneh the Kenizzite and Joshua son of Nun, for they have wholeheartedly followed the LORD" (Numbers 32:11-12).

Caleb and Joshua's steadfast trust excluded them from God's discipline. Imagine being the only older members of the community who would survive the wilderness and live to inherit land in Canaan. This was a testimony to their faith and signifies the high value God places on our confidence and belief in his will for us. When we trust and accept God's will, we are kept from living in the wilderness and permitted to enter the land prepared for us.

REMAINING FAITHFUL

The Israelites knew firsthand of God's powerful arm of protection. He miraculously delivered them from slavery and parted a sea for their escape. His love was expressed in his will for them to possess Canaan. Through their story, we learn that resisting the Lord's will and choosing to rely on ourselves instead of trusting our faithful God can lead to discipline.

- In what ways or circumstances do you find yourself relying on your own understanding instead of trusting God?

- Thoughtfully and prayerfully consider what might keep you from wholeheartedly embracing God's plans.

Lord, truly your will is an expression of your love for me. I know it must grieve you when I refuse to trust you and choose my own way. Surely when I trust I am "as secure as Mount Zion" (Psalm 125:1). You always want what is best for me—and what is best is being in the center of your will. May I grow strong in my faith, my faithfulness, and my obedience. Amen.

The entire experience at Kadesh-Barnea teaches us that there is no substitute for faith in God's promises and obedience to His commandments. Faith is simply obeying God in spite of how we feel, what we see, or what we think might happen.

WARREN WIERSBE, *Be Counted*

uncomfortable grace

*The grace of God has appeared that offers
salvation to all people. It teaches us to say "No"
to ungodliness and worldly passions . . . while we
wait for the blessed hope—the appearing of the
glory of our great God and Savior, Jesus Christ.*

TITUS 2:11-13, NIV

*We all need to teach and encourage one another
with the theology of uncomfortable grace, because
on this side of eternity, God's grace often comes to
us in uncomfortable forms. It may not be what
you and I want, but it is precisely what we need.
God is faithful; he will use the brokenness of the
world that is your present address to complete the
loving work of personal transformation that he has
begun. Now, that's grace!*

PAUL DAVID TRIPP, *New Morning Mercies*

GRACE IS A LOVELY WORD; it promises kindness, favor, and goodwill. The word *discipline*, though, carries the connotation of training, strictness, and correction. Although these words seem unlikely companions, God creatively unites them when he trains and disciplines his children. Certainly it is his unmerited favor that offers and bestows salvation. Our relationship with God begins with his grace and his grace alone. But this unconditional grace he showers upon us spills over into our everyday lives as he purposes to mold and conform us to the image of Christ and to correct us when we sin. Jerry Bridges clarifies this concept:

> What does it mean that God administers His discipline in the realm of grace? It means that all His teaching, training, and discipline are administered in love and for our spiritual welfare. It means that God is never angry with us, though He is often grieved at our sins. It means He does not condemn us or count our sins against us. All that He does in us and to us is done on the basis of unmerited favor.[59]

God's faithfulness to complete the work he began in us can often be viewed as uncomfortable grace—the blending of grace and discipline.

EXPLORING THE WORD

Titus 2:11-12 says that God's grace teaches us to deny sinful and worldly desires. While grace is compassionate, it is also intent on producing godly lives. What aspects of grace are found in these Scriptures?

- Psalm 119:35-40
- Ephesians 1:4-8

LEARNING TO LIVE FAITHFULLY

The melding of God's grace and training are clearly exemplified in the life of the apostle Paul. We've studied the blessing of God's grace for Paul as he lived with a humility-producing thorn, which was sent to counteract potential pride from receiving remarkable revelations from the Lord. When Paul prayed for the thorn's removal, God's answer was, "My grace (My favor and loving-kindness and mercy) is enough for you" (2 Corinthians 12:9, AMPC). The thorn was God's chosen way to care firmly for Paul's soul. Although the thorn was undeniably uncomfortable, it was accompanied by the Lord's empowering grace to endure.

God's discipline of Miriam for challenging Moses' leadership was grounded in grace. Her conduct needed to be called into account; she needed to be reminded to say no to worldly ambition and to live a self-controlled life. Miriam was chastened, swiftly and temporarily. I am sure she would attest to this truth: "No discipline is enjoyable while it is happening—it's painful! But afterward there will be a peaceful harvest of right living for those who are trained in this way" (Hebrews 12:11).

I am grateful for God's faithfulness in wanting to complete his personal work of transformation in me. If I am impatient with someone instead of being kind, the Holy Spirit immediately prompts me to apologize. In this instance God disciplines me. Occasionally, I receive notes from people who express their differing thoughts about my writing. I view God's use of these "thorns" as his method of instilling humility and selflessness in my life. Although his training and discipline are uncomfortable, in my heart of hearts I do not want to be prideful. I do not want to sin and be unaware that I sinned. I want to learn to say no to ungodliness and worldly passion. I want to continually be in the process of becoming more and more like Christ.

God loves us too much to let us alone. He is a faithful Father who desires the highest and best for us, and his intention is to reshape us into wise, righteous, and devoted children who live the faithful way.

REMAINING FAITHFUL

God's discipline is bathed in grace. We are loved, forgiven, and accepted by our Father, but as our Father, he is committed to training and chastening us. We need his uncomfortable grace; it is for our good. Thoughtfully consider the following questions:

- Reflect on a time of discipline or training in your life. What did you sense God wanted to accomplish through this experience?

- In a few sentences, write down what you desire to learn from God's training and discipline.

Father, thank you that your participation in my life is wrapped in your unconditional love and gracious care for my soul. May I wholeheartedly embrace your grace that teaches me to say no to ungodliness and worldly passion, and may I seek to live a self-controlled, upright, and godly life. Teach me to be faithful and to wait with great expectancy for your appearing. Amen.

We see that the very same grace that brings salvation also trains us to live lives that are pleasing to God. All of God's disciplinary processes are grounded in His grace—His unmerited and unconditional favor toward us. We tend to equate discipline with rules and performance standards; God equates it with firm but loving care for our souls.

JERRY BRIDGES, *The Discipline of Grace*

God's faithful forgiveness

Oh, what joy for those
 whose disobedience is forgiven,
 whose sin is put out of sight!
Yes, what joy for those
 whose record the LORD has cleared of guilt,
 whose lives are lived in complete honesty!

PSALM 32:1-2

*Have you started to understand that regardless of
how "bad" you've been or how many times you've
committed the same sin, God completely and freely
forgives you because of Christ? Do you see that,
because God has already dealt with your sins in
Christ, you do not have to do penance or fulfill
some probationary term before God can bless you
or use you again?*

JERRY BRIDGES, *Transforming Grace*

ONE OF MY FRIENDS was unsettled because she had "locked horns" with a colleague at work. She realized that in their exchange of views she had been defensive and unwilling to listen. She was anxious to contact her coworker to ask forgiveness for her insensitivity. Later, my friend called to let me know of the reply she received from her coworker: "No big deal. All is forgiven." She was relieved and grateful. Certainly there is a special consolation for restoration of a relationship and for wrongs pardoned.

Forgiveness on a human level is a cause for rejoicing, but as Maxwell Coder of Moody Bible Institute reminded us, "Human forgiveness simply remits a deserved penalty."[60] On the human level, there is no guarantee we will receive a gracious response. With God, though, we never have to be afraid to approach him or wonder if he will forgive us. Coder continued, "Christ shed His blood for the remission of sins. . . . All who trust in Him as the Lamb of God are forgiven all trespasses, past, present, and future. . . . They are forever delivered from all condemnation."[61]

With a humble heart we acknowledge God's faithful, priceless forgiveness. Oswald Chambers commented, "The heart of salvation is the Cross of Christ. The reason salvation is so easy to obtain is that it cost God so much. The Cross was the place where God and sinful man merged with a tremendous collision and where the way to life was opened. But all the cost and pain of the collision was absorbed by the heart of God."[62] Christ's faithful obedience to sacrifice himself for our sins serves as a powerful motivation to live faithfully.

EXPLORING THE WORD

King David knew all too well the blessing of being forgiven. He proclaimed, "O Lord, you are so good, so ready to forgive, so full of unfailing love for all who ask for your help" (Psalm 86:5). How do these verses help your understanding of God's forgiveness?

- Psalm 32:1-5
- Psalm 51:1-2
- 1 John 1:8-9

LEARNING TO LIVE FAITHFULLY

As a young shepherd, David courageously guarded his father's sheep. These experiences prepared him to be fearless and brave enough to kill the giant Goliath (see 1 Samuel 17:48-51). Chosen to be king of Israel, David composed passionate, forthright psalms of prayer and praise bearing witness to a heart that sought after God.

Later in David's life, at a time when he should have gone to war with his troops, he chose to stay home in Jerusalem. While Uriah, one of David's mighty men, was away fighting his king's battles, Bathsheba, Uriah's wife, caught David's eye. David sent for her, slept with her, and after a few weeks learned that she was pregnant. In an attempt to cover his sin, David requested that Uriah leave the battle, come home, and stay with his wife for a brief period of time. Uriah, though, was a man of integrity and refused to accept this privilege while other soldiers were sleeping in tents on the battlefield. In an ultimate act of treachery, David sent a letter with Uriah instructing the commander to place Uriah in the fiercest part of the battle, and then to withdraw and leave him unprotected, thereby assuring his death (see 2 Samuel 11:1-17).

In a matter of a few weeks, David had shamelessly and blatantly committed adultery and murder—a stunning example of a self-deceived sinner. Eventually God sent Nathan the prophet to confront David: "'Why, then, have you despised the word of the LORD and done this horrible deed? For you have murdered Uriah the Hittite with the sword of the Ammonites and stolen his wife. From this time on, your family will live by the sword because you have despised me by taking Uriah's wife to be your own.' . . . Then David confessed to Nathan, 'I have sinned against the LORD.' Nathan replied, 'Yes, but the LORD has forgiven you, and you won't die for this sin'" (2 Samuel 12:9-10, 13).

So now we have the gift of David's penitential psalms to pray when we are in need of forgiveness. How poignant is David's plea for the Lord to wash him clean from his guilt and purify him from his sin. How moving is his confession—and how touching is his expression of joy in being forgiven. It is incredibly humbling to know that no matter what our sin is or has been, when we confess, God faithfully forgives us.

As Jerry Bridges noted, "God laid our sins on Christ, and He bore the penalty we should have borne. Because of Christ's death in our place, God's justice is now completely satisfied. God can now, without violating His justice or His moral law, forgive us freely, completely and absolutely."[63] Because we are forgiven, we are free to express our gratitude for this priceless gift by living faithfully.

God's forgiveness is a costly gift, freely given. After experiencing God's faithful forgiveness, David prayed in Psalm 51:10, "Create in me a clean heart, O God. Renew a loyal spirit within me." David's response to being forgiven was to be loyal—to be faithful. We must also receive it joyfully, with a humble heart and a desire to express our gratitude through living faithfully.

REMAINING FAITHFUL

David joyfully sang, "The LORD is compassionate and merciful, slow to get angry and filled with unfailing love. . . . He has removed our sins as far from us as the east is from the west" (Psalm 103:8, 12). This gracious forgiveness freely bestowed by our Father does give great joy.

- How does knowing God's forgiveness motivate you to live faithfully?

- As you contemplate the cost and extent of God's forgiveness, express your gratitude for his mercy and love that are bound up in his faithful forgiveness.

―――――――――

Oh Father, there is true joy in knowing the depth and certainty of your forgiveness. I bow before you with profound gratitude for purchasing my freedom and forgiving my sins. Because of your faithful forgiveness, I can live in complete honesty and faithfulness. Amen.

―――――――――

The man who is truly forgiven and knows it, is a man who forgives.

DAVID MARTYN LLOYD-JONES,
Studies in the Sermon on the Mount

facing the consequences

*Your own conduct and actions have brought this
on you.*

JEREMIAH 4:18, NIV

*God in His grace and mercy forgives sin, but in
His divine government He allows that sin to have
its sad effects in the lives of sinners.*

WARREN WIERSBE, *Be Counted*

A LOVELY WOMAN once approached me at a conference and asked if we could talk. After we found a quiet corner, she took a deep breath and shared her story. She was a secretary to a man who was a member of her church. One day they went to lunch together. Frequent lunches led to an affair. She was so enthralled with this relationship that she immediately filed for divorce. Her boss was not as anxious to leave his marriage and was able to reconcile with his wife. This was not the case for my new friend, however, because her husband was too deeply hurt to restore the marriage. This decision left her heartbroken and alone to raise three children. When we met, she was reconciled with God and knew she was forgiven, but she was still carrying the scars of her transgression.

I heard of a pastor who began his sermon one Sunday by saying, "I want everyone here to think about having an affair." After everyone gave a collective gasp, he challenged his congregation, "What I want you to do is to 'play out' the affair to its final conclusion. Carefully consider the repercussions of your choice. Think of the hurt, the brokenness, the pain inflicted on the innocent members who will be affected by an illicit relationship. Think of the consequences before you sin."

I am sure this now-single mom wished she had counted the cost before entering into immorality. She assured me that she wanted others to know of the crushing consequences of sin—consequences that can radically alter your life.

Living faithfully over the course of a lifetime requires

always considering the consequences of our actions. We must face the reality of any decision that would result in unfaithfulness. David, although forgiven of his sin, lived with serious consequences for the rest of his life. Faithfulness does not guarantee agreeable circumstances, but it does promise the Lord's presence, grace, and peace and helps us sidestep the sin that leads to unpleasant circumstances.

EXPLORING THE WORD

Scottish novelist Robert Louis Stevenson observed that sooner or later, everyone sits down to a banquet of consequences.[64] How do these Scriptures confirm this truth, and what do we learn from them about a life of faithfulness?

- Psalm 51:3-4
- 1 Corinthians 3:10-15

LEARNING TO LIVE FAITHFULLY

King David knew the law: "You must not murder. You must not commit adultery. . . . You must not covet your neighbor's wife" (Exodus 20:13-14, 17). So when Nathan reproved him for his sin against Bathsheba and Uriah, it was with considerable comfort and relief that David heard these priceless words: "But the LORD has forgiven you" (2 Samuel 12:13). But along with the message of God's forgiveness, Nathan also had the unpleasant duty of pronouncing the distressing consequences for the king's sin:

> Nathan said to David, . . . "This is what the LORD says: Because of what you have done, I will cause your own household to rebel against you. I will give your wives to another man before your very eyes, and he will go to bed with them in public view. You did it secretly, but I will make this happen to you openly in the sight of all Israel."
>
> Then David confessed to Nathan, "I have sinned against the LORD."
>
> Nathan replied, . . . "Because you have shown utter contempt for the word of the LORD by doing this, your child will die."
>
> 2 SAMUEL 12:7, 11-14

And indeed, we read about the lamentable unfolding of these consequences in Scripture. Four of David's children—Amnon, Absalom, and Tamar, Absalom's sister—played a prominent role in this tragedy. First, David's son by Bathsheba died, as Nathan prophesied. Then, David's eldest son, Amnon, lusted after his half sister, Tamar, and defiled her. David could see his own unbridled passion replicated in Amnon. Choosing to avenge his sister's honor, Absalom murdered Amnon (see 2 Samuel 13). In this, David encountered his own culpability for the murder of Uriah.

We read of Absalom's further treachery when he usurped his father's throne, causing David to flee the city. Nathan's words from the Lord proved true: Absalom rebelled against his father and disgraced his concubines openly (see 2 Samuel 15–16:22).

What devastating and regrettable consequences were set in motion by David's initial sin! The pain of a rebellious household and the death of his child could have been avoided had he exercised self-control and chosen to be faithful. Because he was momentarily tempted, he suffered permanent repercussions.

However, David's repentance is extraordinary. As the Puritan writer Thomas Brooks remarked, "David falls fearfully—but by repentance he rises sweetly."[65] In his psalm of confession David would declare, "Against you, and you alone, have I sinned; I have done what is evil in your sight. You will be proved right in what you say, and your judgment against me is just" (Psalm 51:4). In this insightful prayer, David took responsibility for his conduct and expressed his profound sorrow for the passion that blinded him and for the sin itself that was against God. The discipline was severe, but the king acknowledged that it was justified. To live faithfully before God, we must not only seek to avoid sin but also humbly accept the consequences and repent when we do sin. David prayed, "The sacrifice you desire is a broken spirit. You will not reject a broken and repentant heart, O God" (Psalm 51:17). David graciously faced his consequences, offered a repentant heart, and exemplified the faithful way.

REMAINING FAITHFUL

While we can and should seek faithfulness by proactively considering the consequences of our sin, each of us will sit down to a banquet of consequences at some time in our lives. We must seek to remain faithful even then.

- How does this truth impact your exercise of self-control and the choices that you make?

- How can you seek to live faithfully even in the midst of consequences for sin?

Father, "create in me a clean heart, O God. . . . Restore to me the joy of your salvation, and make me willing to obey you" (Psalm 51:10, 12). Amen.

Give yourself to Him, trust Him, fix your eye upon Him, listen to His voice, and then go on bravely and cheerfully, never doubting for an instant that His grace will lead you in small things as well as great, and will keep you from offending His law of love.

JEAN NICOLAS GROU, *Joy and Strength*

accepting correction

My child, don't reject the LORD's discipline,
  and don't be upset when he corrects you.

PROVERBS 3:11

Chastisement is intended to brace the believer, not
to depress him. Afflictions are the gymnastics of
the spiritual life. They are like the exercises of the
athlete, who is in training for a contest. We are
"exercised thereby" when we accept our troubles
as sent by God himself for our correction; and
when, recognizing this, we cooperate with him in
carrying out their gracious purpose.

C. JERDAN, IN *The Pulpit Commentary*

I LIKE C. JERDAN's unique approach in the previous quote, describing afflictions as "the gymnastics of the spiritual life." These "afflictions," as we view them, are twofold: to correct us when we sin and to train us in Christlikeness. How we respond to God's dealings is decisive in receiving the full intent of the discipline and the resulting formation of our character.

When the Lord told Moses he would not enter Canaan because of his disobedience, Moses petitioned the Lord to reverse the decision. Even though the Lord did not grant his request, Moses graciously accepted correction by obediently commissioning and encouraging Joshua to lead the people (see Deuteronomy 3:21-28). The Lord sent Paul a thorn in the flesh—not to correct him but to train him in humility. Paul also pleaded for the Lord to remove his thorn, but when he was told it served a special purpose, he gladly boasted of this weakness (see 2 Corinthians 12:8-9). King David, when confronted with his sin, asked for forgiveness and prayed for a clean heart and a willingness to obey (see Psalm 51:10, 12).

Self-reliant King Asa, though, who trusted in the king of Aram for deliverance, became so upset when rebuked by Hanani that he threw the prophet into prison and started oppressing some of his people (see 2 Chronicles 16:2-10).

These men exemplify different ways of accepting God's discipline. One way is to choose to be teachable, accept the correction, and be strengthened by the exercise. The other way is to reject God's correction by becoming upset, missing the good the Lord intends to bring into our lives through the discipline—primarily a share in his holiness.

The faithful way embraces and cooperates with the Lord's involvement in our lives. Our faith and trust are in God's love and faithfulness, and his conduct toward us is for our good.

EXPLORING THE WORD

Psalm 119:71 states one of the purposes of chastisement: "My suffering was good for me, for it taught me to pay attention to your decrees." What reasons for accepting God's conduct toward us are given in these verses?

- Romans 5:3-5
- 2 Corinthians 4:16-18

LEARNING TO LIVE FAITHFULLY

Once, when I was traveling from Tucson to Philadelphia for a speaking engagement, a storm in Pennsylvania prompted a two-hour delay in Chicago. After we were finally on our way and approaching the Philadelphia airport, the pilot informed us the weather would prevent an immediate landing, and we would begin to circle until the storm subsided. So began one of my favorite activities while flying! We circled for at least thirty minutes. About every ten minutes the pilot announced, "Ladies and gentlemen, we still do not have permission to land. We will continue to circle. I will keep you updated."

On this flight, I was seated between two men. Each time we were told we could not land, the man on my left became extremely agitated. While looking at his watch, he protested by saying, "I'm never flying this airline again! I'm going to be in rush-hour traffic! I'm going to be late for my meeting." Because our circling was prolonged, the man on my right had to use the white bag in his seat pocket.

I was seated between a man who was angry and a man who was sick. These were my thoughts to the Lord: *Lord, this experience is like life. I'm in a situation I did not choose, and it is certainly an interruption to my plans, but I do have a choice in how I respond: I can decide to be angry because I'm having to suffer and I'm not getting my own way. Or I can choose to allow my circumstances to overwhelm me to the extent that I get sick or lose heart—weary of having to navigate one difficulty after another and just hoping to make it through each day.*

But as I considered these options, this was my prayer: *Father, years ago I gave you my life. It is no longer mine, but yours to use as you please for your glory. And I want you to know that if it pleases you for me to circle Philadelphia, then Lord, it pleases me.*

This particular incident was not one of correction for

sin, but one of training or pruning, such as is mentioned in John 15:2. Jesus taught that God is the gardener who prunes branches to bear more fruit. A. F. Adeney clarified, "All suffering is not chastening. Some trouble is the pruning of branches that already bear fruit, in order that they may bring forth more fruit (John 15:2). But when it meets us in our sins and failings, it is to be regarded as a Divine method of correction."[66] Essentially, correction and pruning and training "feel" the same, though their reasons are different. But each calls for our cooperation in trusting and accepting God's gracious purpose to live faithfully.

REMAINING FAITHFUL

Countless times since my experience on the plane, I have prayed, "Lord, I would not have chosen these present circumstances, but if it pleases you for me to be 'exercised' in this way, then it pleases me." This is my default response in accepting God's interventions in my life; he is training me to remain steadfast in an uncertain world.

- What is your go-to response to training, correction, or troubles in your life?

- What is one decision you can make to be more receptive and teachable when experiencing the Lord's discipline?

Father, thank you for your loving involvement in my life. May I faithfully and joyfully accept and cooperate. Amen.

The object of the discipline is to deliver the subjects of it from sin, to establish them in the faith, and to perfect them in holiness.

W. JONES, IN *The Pulpit Commentary*

DAY 19

watch and pray

Your laws are my treasure;
   they are my heart's delight.
I am determined to keep your decrees
   to the very end.

PSALM 119:111-112

Strenuous care must be taken—watchfulness and
prayer—or else the deceitful heart will wander away.

S. CONWAY, IN *The Pulpit Commentary*

Vince Lombardi, one of the greatest coaches in football history, observed, "It's easy to have faith in yourself and have discipline when you're a winner, when you're number one. What you got to have is faith and discipline when you're not a winner."[67] When we are in the midst of overwhelming or painful circumstances, our untrustworthy hearts can prompt us to take the easy way out. That is when we must remember that choosing faithfulness is to be a continual pursuit.

Joseph certainly understood this. As a rejected brother and a slave in Potiphar's house, he could not be considered a winner. But because of his predetermined decision to remain faithful, he was unwavering. The apostle Paul experienced countless trials, yet he, too, was determined to fight the good fight of faith. He had purposed in his heart to keep God's decrees.

A life of faithfulness requires us to set our hearts on a steadfast commitment to God, but we must also take strenuous care once we have decided to choose faithfulness—care that includes being alert, being intentional, and being prayerful throughout the day.

EXPLORING THE WORD

It was Jesus' last night with his disciples. After the Passover meal, while on the way to the garden of Gethsemane, Jesus predicted that all of the disciples would desert him. Peter's eager, devoted nature impelled him to declare, "Even if everyone else deserts you, I never will." Jesus' reply to Peter was sobering. The Lord said that before the night was over, Peter would deny him. "No!" Peter insisted. "Even if I have to die with you, I will never deny you!" (see Mark 14:29-31). Jesus then took the disciples to the garden to watch and pray. What do you observe in the following passages about Jesus' instructions to his disciples and Peter's subsequent behavior in the courtyard?

- Mark 14:32-38
- Mark 14:66-72

LEARNING TO LIVE FAITHFULLY

We must be forceful and exacting in our commitment to faithfulness, or else our deceitful hearts will lead us astray. Peter's behavior in Mark 14 shows us that! He had been chosen as the leader of the disciples; he was the rock. And it was Peter who first professed Christ as the Messiah. J. R. Thomson commented, "He was no doubt sincere in this bold and confident declaration. But sincerity is not enough; there must be stability as well. . . . Peter's fall is a lesson of caution to the confident and the ardent."[68] We can wholeheartedly desire to be faithful, but we must also cultivate a steadfastness, an enduring nature, a firmness in our commitment.

We see this kind of steadfast, determined faithfulness in Daniel. Daniel, along with others from the noble families of Judah, was taken captive by the Babylonian empire as a young man, and he quickly rose to a high position, serving King Nebuchadnezzar. When King Darius later conquered Babylonia, he appointed Daniel as one of three governors of his kingdom. The other officials became jealous of Daniel's favor and position, and in order to discredit him, they convinced the king to sign a royal decree: For thirty days, any person who prayed to anyone other than the king—divine or human—would be thrown into a lions' den (see Daniel 6:1-9).

But even this threat could not shake Daniel's faithfulness. Incredibly, Daniel, upon hearing of the law, "went home and knelt down as usual in his upstairs room. . . . He prayed three times a day, just as he had always done, giving thanks to his God" (Daniel 6:10). The jealous officials quickly reported his actions to the king. The king tried to rescue Daniel, but the law was irrevocable; Daniel was arrested and thrown into the lions' den. Miraculously, Daniel's faithful God provided an angel to shut the mouths of the lions, and he spent the night in safety—most likely watching and praying (see verses 11-21).

In the garden of Gethsemane, when Jesus asked the disciples to keep watch and pray, Peter's spirit was certainly willing to be faithful—but he neglected prayer and was not on guard against the shrewdness of the enemy. To be watchful is to be attentive, alert, observant, vigilant. Bishop

E. Bickersteth remarked, "Our Lord gives here the true remedy against temptation of every kind; namely, watchfulness and prayer—watchfulness, against the craft and subtlety of the devil or man; and prayer, for the Divine help to overcome."[69]

With the arrest of Jesus, Peter found himself in a very vulnerable position—open to temptation. If we do not take strenuous care to watch, our deceitful hearts will wander away. Faithful watchfulness is a continual watchfulness. As Oswald Chambers noted, "You no more need a day off from spiritual concentration on matters in your life than your heart needs a day off from beating."[70]

Making this determination is all-important; we must set our hearts to pray continually for God's help in overcoming temptation and in attending faithfully to our surroundings. Doing so will allow us to live the faithful way.

REMAINING FAITHFUL

Even though Peter strongly asserted his intent to be faithful, when his faith was put to the test, he denied knowing Jesus before the rooster crowed twice. Someone has suggested the possibility that, after his betrayal, every time Peter heard a rooster crow, he wept—a poignant reminder of his unfaithfulness. But hearing a rooster crow also proclaims a new day, and this was true for Peter. Jesus met him on the shore of the Sea of Galilee and restored him: Peter affirmed his love for the Lord, and Jesus affirmed his love and faith in Peter (see John 21:15-17). Peter experienced the Lord's perfect love and faithful forgiveness and, I believe, began a life of watching and praying.

- What red flags or subtleties of Satan do you need to be aware of that could tempt you to be unfaithful?

- In what specific ways can you take strenuous care to ensure that watchfulness and prayer are a major part of your walk with God?

Father, thank you that you restore and forgive. I pray that I will take strenuous care to remain steadfast. Teach me to be watchful and prayerful in all my circumstances. Amen.

The great lesson . . . is the necessity for humility— that we boast not of our religion, that we presume not on our power; but, in lowly dependence on the strength of Divine grace, walk warily, watching lest we enter into temptation.

R. GREEN, IN *The Pulpit Commentary*

being careful

If you think you are standing strong, be careful not to fall.

I CORINTHIANS 10:12

Always beware of an estimate of life which does not recognise the fact that there is sin.

OSWALD CHAMBERS,

My Utmost for His Highest

IT CONCERNS ME that I can become somewhat comfortable and complacent with the subtleties of sin. I hear about others who have been ensnared by sin and I think, *I would never do that!* But just when we think we are strong, we need to be careful. Scripture is invaluable in alerting us to prideful assumptions.

Phil Ryken, president of Wheaton College, made this observation concerning King David: "A man can be called by God and loved by God, yet still come under sudden attack. A man can trust in God, wait for God, fight for God, sing praise to God, and still give in to a deadly temptation. If it happened to someone as untouchable as David, it could happen to anyone."[71]

No one is exempt from temptation. In our pursuit of living faithfully, we must be intentional in recognizing the fact of sin. As the apostle Peter wrote, "Stay alert! Watch out for your great enemy, the devil. He prowls around like a roaring lion, looking for someone to devour" (1 Peter 5:8). Certainly the devil was like a lion roaring around David, who was not careful to guard his heart and mind when he saw Bathsheba—and failed to remember the reality of sin.

Billy Sunday once said, "One reason that sin flourishes is that it is treated like a cream puff instead of a rattlesnake."[72] If we desire to live faithfully, we must see sin for what it is and be very careful to guard ourselves against it.

EXPLORING THE WORD

It is far too easy for us to trust in our own ability to withstand temptation. We need the teaching and instruction from Scripture to remind us of our vulnerability. What truth do you find in these Scriptures?

- Proverbs 4:23
- Proverbs 16:18
- Proverbs 29:23

LEARNING TO LIVE FAITHFULLY

Perhaps Peter's warning to "stay alert!" was from his own experience; after all, he had failed to recognize the arrogance in his self-confident assertion that he would never desert or deny Jesus. Peter even refuted Jesus' prediction of his denial and condescendingly proclaimed that though the other disciples might fall away, he would remain steadfast. William Osler remarked, "Perhaps no sin so easily besets us as a sense of self-satisfied superiority to others."[73] A major part of being careful is realizing how pride and self-reliance contribute to our susceptibility to sin.

Assuredly pride goes before destruction and haughtiness before a fall. Peter was not careful, and in some way he felt that in his own strength he could withstand sin. It was only after his threefold denial of Jesus that Peter rushed from the courtyard alone and, in his anguish, wept bitterly in repentance.

Solomon is another good example of susceptibility to sin. The Lord appeared to Solomon in a dream and asked him what he wanted. "Wisdom and knowledge" was Solomon's answer (see 2 Chronicles 1:7-10); yet even with this gift of wisdom, he failed to acknowledge the pitfalls of sin. We find these regrettable verses in 1 Kings:

> Now King Solomon loved many foreign women.
> . . . The LORD had clearly instructed the people of
> Israel, "You must not marry them, because they
> will turn your hearts to their gods." Yet Solomon
> insisted on loving them anyway. . . .
>
> In Solomon's old age, they turned his heart to
> worship other gods instead of being completely
> faithful to the LORD his God, as his father, David,
> had been.
>
> I KINGS 11:1-4

Solomon's life ended up being defined by idolatry, sensuality, and a heart set on having its own way. Along with his seven hundred wives and three hundred concubines, he "worshiped Ashtoreth, the goddess of the Sidonians, and Molech, the detestable god of the Ammonites" (1 Kings

11:5). He did not guard his heart with all diligence, he was blind to his pride, and he refused to follow the Lord completely. Herbert Lockyer commented, "The man who penned and preached a thousand wise things failed to practice the wisdom he taught."[74] Oswald Chambers had a brief, yet profound assessment of sin that reminds me of Solomon's life choices: "The essential nature of sin is my claim to my right to myself."[75]

Donald G. Bloesch declared, "Sin, in the evangelical perspective, is not so much the infringement of a moral code as the breaking of a covenantal relationship. Sin is an offense not so much against law as against love. . . . Sin is wounding the very heart of God."[76] How very much we must guard our hearts, be careful, and stay alert to the reality of sin, our pride, and self-dependence. If we desire a lifetime of faithfulness, we should take to heart 1 Corinthians 10:12: "Let him who thinks he is standing securely beware of falling" (WNT). We must live in the Spirit and keep in step with the Spirit. As Bloesch wisely reminds us, "We become most aware of our sinfulness in the presence of the holy God."[77]

REMAINING FAITHFUL

Thomas Carlyle stated, "The greatest fault is to be conscious of none."[78] One way sin beguiles us is by making us think we are immune to certain sins. A man who was in an accountability group once shared that he would never commit adultery—and only six weeks later, he did. Being careful to recognize the deceptiveness of sin is a lifelong but essential task for living faithfully.

- What lessons about faithfulness and guarding against sin do you learn from Peter and Solomon?

- In what ways can you become more aware and more sensitive to the reality of sin?

"Search me, O God, and know my heart; test me and know my anxious thoughts. Point out anything in me that offends you, and lead me along the path of everlasting life" (Psalm 139:23-24). Amen.

Measure your growth in grace by your sensitiveness to sin.

OSWALD CHAMBERS,
IN *The Westminster Collection of Christian Quotations*

hindrances to living the faithful way

Who can discern his errors?
    Declare me innocent from hidden faults.
Keep back your servant also from presumptuous sins;
    let them not have dominion over me!
Then I shall be blameless,
    and innocent of great transgression.

PSALM 19:12-13, ESV

One of the most fundamental truths we must learn
in Christian growth is that we are responsible,
yet dependent. That is, we are responsible to obey
God's commands. We are responsible for our sin.
We cannot blame the devil or other people. . . . We
do not obey because we choose not to obey. Yet at
the same time we do not have the resources within
ourselves to obey. We are completely dependent
upon the Holy Spirit.

JERRY BRIDGES, *I Will Follow You, O God*

UZZIAH WAS SIXTEEN YEARS OLD when he ascended to the throne of Judah. While he is remembered for ruling during an era of prosperity, he is also remembered for his sin. Scripture tells us his sad story: "As long as the king sought guidance from the LORD, God gave him success. . . . But when he had become powerful, he also became proud, which led to his downfall. He sinned against the LORD his God by entering the sanctuary of the LORD's Temple and personally burning incense on the incense altar" (2 Chronicles 26:5, 16). When Uzziah was confronted and reproved by the priests, he became furious. But as he stood in the Temple raging at the priests, he was struck with leprosy and had it until the day he died (see 2 Chronicles 26:19, 21). Herbert Lockyer remarked, "This Uzziah is a blazing warning against the spiritual pride that brings presumption."[79]

King David, the author of Psalm 19, earnestly prayed for the Lord to become involved in his life so that he could remain blameless. He asked God to cleanse him from hidden faults—sins that God saw but were essentially unknown to David. Hidden sins can be thought of as sins we commit in secret, but David's plea addressed his concern about committing sins unknowingly: "How can I know all the sins lurking in my heart?" (verse 12). Indeed, hidden faults lurk in our deceitful hearts and need to be brought to our attention and cleansed.

David then implored God to deliver him from presumptuous sins. For me, just to pronounce the word *presumptuous* conveys its meaning: willful, insolent, audacious, impudent. The word itself sounds so arrogant! Uzziah exemplified presumptuous sin. He thought he was above the law. His sin was intentional and deliberate. Concerned about the sin of presumption, David appealed for the Lord's restraining grace to keep him free from guilt and innocent of great sin.

Only as we seek to have our hidden faults exposed can we stay on the faithful path. Praying as David did for freedom from blind spots keeps us dependent on and sensitive to the Holy Spirit. We must eliminate any hindrances to pursuing a life of faithfulness.

EXPLORING THE WORD

Included in Psalm 19 is David's praise of God's Word: "The commands of the LORD are clear, giving insight for living" (verse 8). How do the following Scriptures help us understand sin in relation to God?

- Numbers 15:30-31
- Psalm 65:3
- Hebrews 4:13

LEARNING TO LIVE FAITHFULLY

How much we need to be made aware of the small, unnoticed sins that hide in our hearts. We likely all know individuals who frequently wound people by their words or actions but are oblivious to the hurts they have inflicted. One of my continual prayers is that I would never sin without knowing it. Often the Holy Spirit will "speak to my heart" concerning my insensitivity toward others. My intent is never to harm anyone, so I'm grateful to be shown my hidden faults and most thankful for the cleansing I receive when I acknowledge and repent of my errors.

Robert Sanderson, an English bishop in the 1600s, made these observations concerning the sins of three prominent men of Scripture: "Paul's persecution [of the church was] a grievous sin, yet a sin of ignorance; Peter's denial a grievous sin, yet a sin of infirmity [or weakness]; David's murder, a far more grievous sin than either of both, because [it was] a sin of presumption."[80] David's sin was deliberate and premeditated in its execution, therefore it was presumptuous.

The circumstances that prompted David to write Psalm 19 are unknown, but regardless of the timing, David knew the power and devastation of presumptuous sin. His ardent petition was for God to prevent him, hold him back, stop him from committing deliberate sins and save him from the dominance such sins can command. David asked for God's control and professed his dependence and full reliance upon the Lord. Despite David's sin against Bathsheba and Uriah, I think this prayer is evidence that he was a man after God's own heart.

We find in 1 John 3:9 that "those who have been born into God's family do not make a practice of sinning, because God's life is in them." We need to remember that we still have to deal with our flesh, and we will sin, but as God's children we do not make a *practice* of sin—we do not premeditate sin. When we do transgress, though, we are accountable for our sin and responsible to confess it. The great deterrent to sin is sensitivity to the checks and impressions of the Spirit that keep us from wrongdoing. We are responsible, but we also have the glorious privilege of being completely dependent on the power of the Holy Spirit to live faithfully.

REMAINING FAITHFUL

Psalm 119:133 is a good verse to pray as we seek to guard against hidden and presumptuous sins: "Direct my footsteps according to your word; let no sin rule over me" (NIV). Our God is indeed faithful, and we find our ever-present help through his Spirit and his Word.

- Take time to prayerfully ask God to search your heart in regard to hidden faults or an inclination to be presumptuous.

- How would you describe your dependence on the Holy Spirit for his power to live blamelessly and faithfully?

Father, reveal my hidden faults and keep me from presumptuous sin. May I learn to completely depend upon the Holy Spirit. Amen.

When we choose deliberately to obey Him, then He will tax the remotest star and the last grain of sand to assist us.

OSWALD CHAMBERS, *My Utmost for His Highest*

temptation-aware

The temptations in your life are no different from what others experience. And God is faithful. He will not allow the temptation to be more than you can stand. When you are tempted, he will show you a way out so that you can endure.

1 CORINTHIANS 10:13

Because the world you live in isn't operating as per God's original design, it presents you with temptations everywhere you live. . . . You and I must live temptation-aware; to fail to do so is to fail to recognize the fallenness of the world that happens to be the address where we live.

PAUL DAVID TRIPP, *New Morning Mercies*

IN INDONESIA the natives used to catch monkeys by boring a hole in a coconut and dropping in a pebble. They would wait for a monkey to pick up the coconut, rattle it, and place his hand in the opening to retrieve the rock. The opening was so small that he'd be unable to bring his hand and the pebble out at the same time—and the monkey was easy prey. A nun shared this story with Brother Andrew before he became a Christian, and he later became famous for smuggling Bibles into countries during the Cold War. She was confronting him about his foolhardy lifestyle of yielding to temptation, which kept him from being free.[81]

Temptation is enticement to sin. Biblical commentator E. Hurndall wrote, "Temptation is not compulsion. . . . Temptation at its strongest is only *inducement*. . . . Every sin we commit is voluntary. Sin is consent to the temptation."[82] James confirms this thought: "Temptation comes from our own desires, which entice us and drag us away" (James 1:14). Giving in to temptation is placing our hand in the coconut.

We live in a temptation-filled world—one that lies in the power of the evil one (see 1 John 5:19). But God has not left us helpless in the face of our enemies. Romans 13:14 tells us, "Clothe yourself with the presence of the Lord Jesus Christ. And don't let yourself think about ways to indulge your evil desires." Clothing ourselves with the Lord is a picture of abiding in Christ. I believe that as we stay connected to Christ and clothe ourselves with him, we become fully armored.

Concerning the armor, Paul wrote, "Be strong in the Lord and in his mighty power. Put on all of God's armor so that you will be able to stand firm against all strategies of the devil" (Ephesians 6:10-11). As we examine the armor of God (see verses 13-17), we find that Jesus and his Word are truth; Jesus gives peace; Jesus is the one who gives salvation; and the sword of the Spirit is the Word of God. Jesus is also the author and perfecter of our faith (see Hebrews 12:2). In clothing ourselves with Christ, daily abiding in his presence, we are fully armored and equipped to resist sin and obey the Spirit's leading in escaping temptation.

EXPLORING THE WORD

In Psalm 119:133 the psalmist prayed, "Guide my steps by your word, so I will not be overcome by evil." In the following Scriptures, what truths do you discover about responding to temptation?

- Psalm 141:4-5
- 1 Peter 5:8-11
- 2 Peter 2:9

LEARNING TO LIVE FAITHFULLY

The Holy Spirit desires holiness and is faithful to show a way out of temptation so that we can endure and remain faithful.

As we put on God's armor through abiding, we indicate our dependence and intent on following the Spirit. Here are a few ways of escape:

- *Obey the Word.* "Put to death the sinful, earthly things lurking within you. Have nothing to do with sexual immorality, impurity, lust, and evil desires" (Colossians 3:5).

- *Know and quote Scripture.* Jesus countered each of Satan's temptations by quoting Scripture (see Matthew 4:4, 7, 10). The Word is the sword of the Spirit, the offensive weapon in spiritual warfare.

- *Flee.* "Run from anything that stimulates youthful lusts" (2 Timothy 2:22). "Don't do as the wicked do, and don't follow the path of evildoers. Don't even think about it; don't go that way. Turn away and keep moving" (Proverbs 4:14-15). This is what Joseph did. Remember, in his haste to run away from Potiphar's wife, "he left his cloak in her hand" (Genesis 39:12). Thomas Brooks reminds us, "God will not remove the temptation, except you turn from the occasion."[83] Let's put away the questionable book, leave the explicit movie, and forsake anything that promotes sinful thoughts or behaviors.

- *Watch and pray.* Jesus encouraged the disciples, "Watch and pray so that you will not fall into temptation. The spirit is willing, but the flesh is weak" (Matthew 26:41,

NIV). Jesus also taught us to pray, "Don't let us yield to temptation, but rescue us from the evil one" (Matthew 6:13). This petition echoes David's prayer for God to restrain him from deliberate sin. Jesus knows the temptations we face: "This High Priest of ours understands our weaknesses, for he faced all of the same testings we do, yet he did not sin. So let us come boldly to the throne of our gracious God. There we will receive his mercy, and we will find grace to help us when we need it most" (Hebrews 4:15-16).

- *Practice godly fellowship.* Those with whom we associate have a powerful influence on our responses to temptation. First Corinthians 15:33 says, "Do not be deceived: 'Bad company ruins good morals'" (ESV). And Paul wrote to Timothy, "Enjoy the companionship of those who call on the Lord with pure hearts" (2 Timothy 2:22). Godly fellowship is invaluable in encouraging us to be faithful.

- *Submit to God and resist Satan.* James 4:7 tells us, "Humble yourselves before God. Resist the devil, and he will flee from you." Through the power of the Holy Spirit, his Word, and our dependence on him, we can stand firm against Satan, confident of a way of escape.

REMAINING FAITHFUL

Erwin Lutzer made a wise observation: "Temptation is not sin, it is a call to battle."[84] We fight by being alert, by being fully armored, and by being willing to follow the Holy Spirit toward a way out of the temptation.

- What can you do to become more temptation-aware?

- Which "ways of escape" best help you in dealing with temptation?

Father, again I am humbled by your provision in helping me live in this sinful world. May I live temptation-aware. Amen.

Thou wilt not displease thy best and greatest friend [God], by yielding to his greatest enemy.

THOMAS BROOKS,
Precious Remedies against Satan's Devices

DAY 23

faithful fellowship

*Run from anything that stimulates youthful lusts.
Instead, pursue righteous living, faithfulness, love,
and peace. Enjoy the companionship of those who
call on the Lord with pure hearts.*

2 TIMOTHY 2:22

*We thank God for human companionship; we
rejoice greatly that he has so "fashioned our hearts
alike," and so interwoven our human lives, that
we can be much to one another, and do much for
one another, as we go on our way.*

W. CLARKSON, IN *The Pulpit Commentary*

I LIKE JOHN WILLISON's thoughts on friendship: "Make the liveliest of God's people your greatest intimates, and see that their love and likeness to Christ be the great motive of your love to them, more than their love or likeness to you."[85] Part of our purpose in forming godly friendships should be to pursue righteous living and faithfulness together. As we enjoy like-hearted fellowship, we are strengthened in our commitment and devotion to Christ. And of course it is an extra-special blessing when our friends are "lively"!

The pursuit of faithfulness, love, and peace forged the unlikely friendship that we find in the Bible between Jonathan and David. Jonathan, son of King Saul, was the heir apparent to the throne, but David was God's chosen successor. Yet their hearts were drawn together in a special friendship. When the two men first met, we are told, "there was an immediate bond between them, for Jonathan loved David" (1 Samuel 18:1). As Gary Inrig wrote, "The essence of Jonathan and David's friendship is that it went beyond superficial attraction to spiritual attraction. Their souls were knit together."[86]

When David became a fugitive, persistently hunted by a jealous King Saul, Jonathan risked the wrath of his father and went to David. He "encouraged him to stay strong in his faith in God," telling him, "Don't be afraid" (see 1 Samuel 23:16-17). One of the blessings of friendship is having someone who willingly comes with words of encouragement to stay strong and faithful in the midst of turmoil. As Proverbs 17:17 says, "A friend loves at all times" (ESV), and faithful friends comfort us and strengthen us to live faithfully.

EXPLORING THE WORD

Our friendship with Jesus prepares us to be good friends to others. As we abide in Christ, we receive and partake of Jesus' love, and it is his love in us that we share. What do you observe about the importance of fellowship in these Scriptures?

- Ecclesiastes 4:9-12
- Hebrews 10:24-25

LEARNING TO LIVE FAITHFULLY

When I think about friendship, what comes to mind are things like laughter, fun, and enjoyment with someone who cares for me. But while it is worthwhile to share good times together, true spiritual friendship goes far deeper and involves mutual counsel, reproof, and accountability. The book of Ecclesiastes emphasizes the value and necessity of having other people in our lives; we each need individuals who care about who we are, what we are doing, and how faithfully we are following the Lord. Here are some specific ways spiritual friendship can enrich our lives:

- *Accountability.* Hebrews 3:13 says, "You must warn each other every day, while is still 'today,' so that none of you will be deceived by sin and hardened against God." As we have discovered, spiritual pitfalls and the subtle enticements of sin exist all around us. We are responsible for our obedience, but how good it is to have someone "looking over our shoulder" to alert us to the deception of sin. No one enjoys being reproved, but true friendship considers the other's welfare. We see this in Paul's confrontation of Peter, which Paul wrote about in Galatians: Peter had stopped eating with Gentile Christians because he was "afraid of criticism" from Jewish Christians, and Paul strongly warned Peter about the hypocrisy of such behavior (see Galatians 2:11-13).

- *Strong counsel.* Colossians 3:16 says, "Let the message about Christ, in all its richness, fill your lives. Teach and counsel each other with all the wisdom he gives." The rich dwelling of Christ's Word in our hearts is the basis for teaching and counseling. We seek counsel from those who call on the Lord with a pure heart and who use the Word and prayer in their teaching and guidance. And Proverbs 27:9 tells us, "The heartfelt counsel of a friend is as sweet as perfume and incense."

- *Encouragement.* Hebrews 10:24 encourages, "Let us think of ways to motivate one another to acts of love and good works." A friend will bring out the best in you—love, kindness, and service. One day I was having lunch with a good friend, and when we asked for our bill, we were told it had already been paid. A very kind person made our day by encouraging and motivating us through their love and good works.

- *Faithful wounds.* Proverbs 27:6 says, "Faithful are the wounds of a friend, but deceitful are the kisses of an enemy" (NASB). These are difficult words. No one enjoys being reproved, but true friendship considers the welfare of another. This was true of Nathan, who as a royal adviser to David "faithfully wounded" his king when he confronted him about his sin. Joseph Hall, Bishop of Norwich, challenged us with these thoughts: "Christians should 'speak the truth in love.' . . . If the erring one does not learn it from the lips of love, he will have to learn it from a harsher source and in ruder tones. . . . There cannot be a more worthy improvement of friendship than in a fervent opposition to the sins of those we love."[87] How we respond to reproof indicates how wise we are, as we see in Proverbs 9:8: "Correct the wise, and they will love you." I am learning to be thankful when someone points out a blind spot in my life for, truth be told, I don't want to sin without knowing it. And I am especially grateful when I am told I have spinach in my teeth!

REMAINING FAITHFUL

Like David, we all need "Nathans" in our lives to hold us accountable and speak truth to us, and we need "Jonathans" to give us encouragement and support. We need the enjoyment of friends who call on the Lord with pure hearts and who desire to live the faithful way.

- As you think about your friends, how would you evaluate the depth of your relationships in terms of accountability and encouragement to walk with God?

- Take time to pray for friends who will love you enough to speak truth into your life.

Father, I thank you for true friends. May I be a faithful friend, and may I fully embrace those who pursue righteousness, faithfulness, love, and peace. Amen.

I am a friend to anyone who fears you—anyone who obeys your commandments.

PSALM 119:63

a disciplined athlete

Don't you realize that in a race everyone runs, but only one person gets the prize? So run to win! All athletes are disciplined in their training. They do it to win a prize that will fade away, but we do it for an eternal prize.

1 CORINTHIANS 9:24-25

So live; so deny yourselves; so make constant exertion, that you may not fail of that prize, the crown of glory, which awaits the righteous in heaven.

ALBERT BARNES,
Barnes' Notes on the Whole Bible

AROUND AD 54, while Paul was in Ephesus, he wrote a letter to the Corinthian church in which he alluded to their famous biennial Isthmian Games (see 1 Corinthians 9:24-27). These contests were celebrated with extraordinary pomp and splendor, and at this time they overshadowed the Olympic Games.

Paul used the Corinthians' familiarity with the games to compare an athlete's discipline of his body to win a temporary prize with the daily diligence believers should exert over their bodies to pursue an eternal prize: "I run with purpose in every step. I am not just shadowboxing. I discipline my body like an athlete, training it to do what it should. Otherwise, I fear that after preaching to others I myself might be disqualified" (1 Corinthians 9:26-27).

As we seek to live faithful lives, we must discipline our sinful flesh and, as Paul exhorts, run the race with purpose and persistence in order to overcome the deeds of our sinful nature.

We know of God's justifying and sanctifying work in our lives, and we can consider ourselves dead to the power of sin, but we still have to contend with our flesh. Martyn Lloyd-Jones commented, "Our spirits are already entirely delivered from sin. I . . . as a spiritual being, am dead to sin. I have finished with it once and for ever, but that is not true of my body."[88] In Romans 8:23 we read, "We believers also groan, even though we have the Holy Spirit within us as a foretaste of future glory, for we long for our bodies to be released from sin and suffering." Often we complain about our bodies, but we are not left helpless; we have the Holy Spirit's strength and support to live the faithful way.

EXPLORING THE WORD

C. Lipscomb wrote, "*Ideally*, the body is the soul's helper. . . . *Practically*, the body is so sensitive to itself, so in love with its own enjoyments, so enslaved to its lusts and appetites, that it must be kept under and brought into subjection."[89] Read the following verses and record what additional teaching you discover about managing your flesh:

- Romans 8:5-10
- Ephesians 5:3-4

LEARNING TO LIVE FAITHFULLY

It is valuable for me to understand the responsibility I have in disciplining my body. Yes, I have the Holy Spirit to prompt and empower me, but I must "run with purpose in every step." Being careful and intentional is crucial. Paul gave these instructions to the Roman church: "Dear brothers and sisters, I plead with you to give your bodies to God because of all he has done for you. Let them be a living and holy sacrifice—the kind he will find acceptable. This is truly the way to worship him" (Romans 12:1). To be a living and holy sacrifice is a graphic illustration of what it looks like to discipline our bodies.

Albert Barnes explained,

> We are to present ourselves with all our living, vital energies. Christianity does not require a service of death or inactivity. It demands vigorous and active powers in the service of God the Saviour. There is something very affecting in this view for such a sacrifice; in regarding life, with all its energies, its intellectual, and moral, and physical powers, as one long *sacrifice*; one continued offering unto God.[90]

To be a living sacrifice implies that we discipline and exercise our energies to do as God wills. This sacrifice is voluntary—we place ourselves on the altar and with our whole being offer ourselves in worship. Our race is lifelong, and so is our sacrifice.

To be a living and *holy* sacrifice takes strict discipline. Paul's fear of disqualification was real. It takes vigilance, commitment, and perseverance to be holy, but we do not fight this battle alone. We have this encouragement from Philippians 2:12-13: "Work hard to show the results of your salvation, obeying God with deep reverence and fear. For God is working in you, giving you the desire and the power to do what pleases him." As commentator R. Finlayson wrote, "From the *crucified* and exalted Savior, through the Spirit, God puts forth power to *counteract* the weakness of our will, to give it power in choosing the good and refusing evil."[91]

We are empowered by God to go through our days deliberately choosing good and refusing evil. Our primary purpose in disciplining ourselves to remain faithful is to express our love and gratitude to God for all he has done for us.

REMAINING FAITHFUL

Like disciplined athletes, we must commit to offering ourselves as living sacrifices and our bodies as instruments of righteousness in response to God's love and faithfulness and his promised eternal prize.

- How would you describe your daily spiritual exercise routine that enables you to present your body as a living sacrifice?

- What ultimately motivates you to run toward the eternal prize?

Father, thank you for freeing me from the power of sin and enabling me to do your good pleasure. May I present my body in loving obedience as an act of worship. Amen.

Christ teaches us to honour the body that God's wonder working hand has framed, and that he makes the temple of his Spirit. But then do we most honour the body when we make it most thoroughly the submissive servant of the soul's diviner purposes, confronting it, meeting it full in the face, as it were, with the sweet violence of our holy purpose, when it dares to obstruct the spirit in its path to the heavenly crown.

J. WAITE, IN *The Pulpit Commentary*

eeping in step with the Spirit

If we live by the Spirit, let us also keep in step with the Spirit.

GALATIANS 5:25, ESV

We may consult and know his will, if (1) we intelligently and devoutly study his Word, (2) unselfishly regard the leadings of his providence, (3) earnestly ask for the promptings of his Divine Spirit.

W. CLARKSON, IN *The Pulpit Commentary*

If we are to keep in step with the Spirit and allow him to lead, then it is helpful to understand exactly how the Holy Spirit works in us. William Evans explained the Spirit's work in this way:

> We may speak of the baptism of the Spirit as that initial act of the Spirit by which, at the moment of our regeneration, we are baptized by the Spirit into the body of Christ; the Spirit then comes and takes up His dwelling within the believer. The filling with the Spirit, however, is not confined to one experience or to any one point of time exclusively; it may be repeated times without number.[92]

Paul instructs believers not to be drunk with wine but to "instead, be filled with the Holy Spirit" (Ephesians 5:18). Warren Wiersbe gives this clarification: "'Be filled with the Spirit' is God's command. . . . The verb is in the present tense—'keep on being filled'—so it is an experience we should enjoy constantly and not just on special occasions. . . . To be 'filled with the Spirit' means to be constantly controlled by the Spirit in our mind, emotions, and will."[93]

Yielding to the Spirit's leadership and setting our hearts to be intentionally faithful will keep us from quenching or stifling the Spirit's control (see 1 Thessalonians 5:19) or grieving him by the way we live (see Ephesians 4:30). When we are filled with the Holy Spirit, he enables us to respond properly to the flesh and to stay on a faithful, obedient path. We become more aware of his presence and more sensitive to his promptings. As English hymn writer and theologian Frederick W. Faber taught, "God always fills in all hearts all the room which is left Him there."[94]

EXPLORING THE WORD

Our ongoing relationship with the Spirit in humble dependence will empower us to remain faithful. Read these verses and record what you learn about the Holy Spirit:

- John 16:13-15
- 1 Corinthians 2:12
- 1 John 3:24

LEARNING TO LIVE FAITHFULLY

"God speaks by His Spirit through His Word. Sometimes He speaks directly without the written word. But *very, very rarely*. The mental impressions by which the Spirit guides are frequent."[95]

This thought by S. D. Gordon on how the Spirit leads is most helpful to me. Certainly, the Holy Spirit who moved in the hearts of men to write the Scriptures will always use his Word to teach and guide us. I like W. Clarkson's admonition to study the Scriptures intelligently and devotedly. After all, as Paul instructed Timothy, "all Scripture is inspired by God and is useful to teach us what is true and to make us realize what is wrong in our lives. It corrects us when we are wrong and teaches us to do what is right" (2 Timothy 3:16). With such a promise, why would we not devote ourselves to the study of Scripture and allow the Word to teach and correct us?

The Spirit uses numerous verses to help keep me in step with him. One he uses frequently is Ephesians 4:2: "Always be humble and gentle. Be patient with each other, making allowance for each other's faults because of your love." Another is 1 John 2:6: "Those who say they live in God should live their lives as Jesus did." What a straightforward challenge to stay faithful!

William Evans wrote that the Spirit often guides through mental impressions. I do sense the Spirit's leading through the "nudges" he gives. I like to say, "His thoughts are in my heart."

One guideline for recognizing the promptings of the Spirit is that he will never lead in a way that is contrary to his Word. We are to check out strong impulses we might have to be sure they agree with Scripture. I know when an impression is the work of the Holy Spirit, because what he is impressing upon me conforms to Scripture, it is pleasing to God, it is something I know I should do, and I have a settled peace about it. Usually I'm prompted to apologize to someone, spend time encouraging a friend, or refrain from reading or watching something that is not edifying.

Fairly recently I was asked to disciple two women who were longtime friends. While it was very special to be together, it became increasingly difficult to find a mutually agreeable time for all three of us to meet. I was willing to meet sporadically, but the Spirit impressed upon me to meet with them separately. Now, I would not have thought of that solution because of their close friendship and desire to be together. I was concerned about their response, but I felt led to offer this option. We met and they agreed to this plan. The Spirit knew what would be best for all of us, and indeed it has been.

A wise person once said, "To know the will of God, you should have no will of your own." This is true as we seek to keep in step with the Spirit. Jesus taught that the Holy Spirit leads us into all truth (see John 14:17). To live faithfully, we must cast aside our own wills and earnestly ask for the promptings of the Divine Spirit. We should always allow the Holy Spirit to have the final say if we want to walk in the way of faithfulness.

REMAINING FAITHFUL

Erwin Lutzer, pastor of Moody Church in Chicago, wrote, "To be controlled by the Spirit means that we are not controlled by what happens on the outside but by what is happening on the inside."[96] The key to keeping in step with the Spirit is being responsive to his inner promptings.

- What is one thing you can do to become more sensitive to the Holy Spirit?

- How do you sense the Spirit's leading and presence?

Father, thank you for the empowering work of the Holy Spirit. May I keep in step and be sensitive, alert, and quick to obey. Amen.

Well, that One who resides within the heart is very sensitive and is very faithful. If I will jealously keep on good terms, aye on the best terms, with Him, ever listening, ever obeying, I will come to know at first touch the thing that disturbs His sensitive spirit.

S. D. GORDON, *Quiet Talks on Power*

abiding in the Word

I am the vine; you are the branches. Whoever abides in me and I in him, he it is that bears much fruit, for apart from me you can do nothing.

JOHN 15:5, ESV

How does the branch bear fruit? Not by incessant effort for sunshine and air, not by vain struggles. . . . It simply abides in the vine, in silent and undisturbed union, and blossoms, and fruit appear as of spontaneous growth. How then shall a Christian bear fruit? By efforts and struggles to obtain that which is freely given? . . . No: there must be a full concentration of the thoughts and affections on Christ, a complete surrender of the whole being to Him, a constant looking to Him for grace.

HARRIET BEECHER STOWE,

How to Live on Christ

OFTEN WHEN I SPEAK at a conference, I share about Jesus visiting the home of Martha, Mary, and Lazarus. Martha was busy in the kitchen, preparing the meal, but Mary was sitting at the feet of Jesus, listening to what he taught. Martha, distracted by her serving, went to Jesus and complained about Mary not helping her. "But the Lord said to her, 'My dear Martha, you are worried and upset over all these details! There is only one thing worth being concerned about. Mary has discovered it, and it will not be taken away from her'" (Luke 10:41-42).

What amazes me about Jesus' reply is his declaration that "there is only one thing worth being concerned about." I like it when I'm told there is only "one" thing to do; I like the bottom line. Here we have the Lord giving us an essential element of walking with him: sitting at his feet and listening to his Word. In his response to Martha, the Lord is declaring the need for right priorities. Our highest desire should be to seek first the Kingdom of God, so that we bear Christlike character and serve at his prompting and direction. That's what we see as well in Jesus' description of a branch staying connected to the vine. Maintaining a secure attachment to the Lord is of utmost spiritual importance.

Abiding with Jesus equips us to bear the fruit of the Spirit, the foundation of the faithful life. That's why our devotional life is indispensable; it is the one choice we need to make each day. If abiding in him is not our main concern, then Jesus warns us that anything we do apart from him will result in nothing—nothing of eternal value that will bring glory to God.

EXPLORING THE WORD

Regarding the value of God's Word, Peter wrote, "No prophecy in Scripture ever came from the prophet's own understanding, or from human initiative. No, those prophets were moved by the Holy Spirit, and they spoke from God" (2 Peter 1:20-21). What added insights about the importance of the Word can we learn from these verses?

- Psalm 119:105
- 2 Timothy 3:16-17

LEARNING TO LIVE FAITHFULLY

A branch bears fruit by simply abiding. Christians, though, must be wholeheartedly committed to abiding—to concentrating our thoughts and affections on Christ. Just as Martha was distracted by her preparations, we, too, can be easily drawn away from our time with the Lord. Jesus highlighted this truth in the parable of the farmer scattering seed: "As for what was sown among thorns, this is the one who hears the word, but the cares of the world and the deceitfulness of riches choke the word, and it proves unfruitful" (Matthew

13:22, ESV). How very true. Countless days I have allowed the cares of the world to choke out the Word.

One day John 15:5 penetrated my heart: "Yes, I am the vine; you are the branches. Those who remain in me, and I in them, will produce much fruit. For apart from me you can do nothing." I thought, *I don't want to go through life doing nothing for the Lord, so if there is only one thing to be concerned about and that is abiding in Christ, then I want to make abiding the priority in my life.* My definition of abiding is consistently sitting at the feet of Jesus, listening to his Word with a heart to obey.

Pastor R. A. Torrey challenged, "If we are to obtain from God all that we ask from Him, Christ's words must abide or continue in us. We must study His words, fairly devour His words, let them sink into our thought and into our heart, keep them in our memory, obey them constantly in our life, let them shape and mold our daily life and our every act. This is really the method of abiding in Christ."[97] Having a Bible reading plan has really encouraged me to be consistent in my devotional life. If I miss a day or two, I do not try to catch up but just begin reading the Scriptures for the present day. I take encouragement from what Samuel Gordon wrote: "[Spend] time alone with the book daily. It should be unhurried time. Time enough not to think about time."[98]

I cannot imagine attempting to live faithfully without the blessing of abiding. Being still before God allows the Lord to speak to us through his Word, which is alive and active and exposes our innermost thoughts and desires. It is in this quiet time that we are less engaged with the world and more receptive to hearing from God and seeking his guidance for the faithful way. It is the "one thing worth being concerned about" if we desire to be faithful.

REMAINING FAITHFUL

I cannot think of a more perfect plan for bearing fruit than just sitting at the feet of Jesus, listening to his Word, and becoming more and more intimate with him. How can we neglect so great an honor?

- How would you describe the importance of abiding in your relationship with the Lord?

- In what ways can you strengthen your abiding and your love for God's Word?

Father, may I treasure your Word and daily take time to sit at your feet so that any fruit I bear will honor you and bless others. May my abiding be the joy of my life. Amen.

We are spiritually united to the Saviour. We become one with him. . . . It is a union of feeling and affection; a union of principle and of congeniality; a union of dependence as well as love; a union where nothing is to be imparted by us, but everything gained.

ALBERT BARNES,
Barnes' Notes on the New Testament

faithful in prayer

*Devote yourselves to prayer with an alert mind
and a thankful heart.*

COLOSSIANS 4:2

*How then can we grow in a conscious sense of
dependence on Christ? Through the discipline of
prayer. Prayer is the tangible expression of our
dependence. We may assent to the fact that we
are dependent on Christ, but if our prayer life is
meager or perfunctory, we thereby deny it. We are
in effect saying we can handle most of our spiritual
life with our own self-discipline and our perceived
innate goodness.*

JERRY BRIDGES, *Growing Your Faith*

A TEENAGE SOLDIER in the Chinese Red Guard once tuned in to a Christian radio broadcast. Finding it interesting, he made a habit of listening. As the truth about Jesus sank into his heart, he became a believer in Christ. In a letter that was smuggled out and delivered to the station, he asked two questions: "Can God accept somebody without a church?" and "Would you please teach me to pray? . . . I would like to pray, but I don't know how." He had no one to teach him about prayer, but "he imagined prayer meant, 'to speak the whole day so that after everything you say, you might be able to add 'Amen.'"[99]

I so appreciate this distinctive view of prayer! This young man's story shows us the continual awareness we should have of God's presence as we walk with him throughout the day. Faithfulness in prayer allows us to grow in our dependence upon and intimacy with the Lord and acknowledges our need to rely on him to live a faithful life.

Over the years, I have discovered that prayer is not just an opportunity to relate all my concerns to the Lord but also an opportunity for the Lord to minister to me as well. Martin Smith wisely reminds us of these easily forgotten aspects of prayer: "What if prayer is a means of God nourishing, restoring, healing, converting us? Suppose prayer is primarily allowing ourselves to be loved, addressed and claimed by God. . . . What if our part in prayer is primarily letting God be giver?"[100] This perspective on prayer encourages me to have more than a meager or perfunctory prayer life. God-nourished, restorative prayer is a necessary and powerful gift given to us to help us stay on the faithful path.

EXPLORING THE WORD

Paul instructed the Colossians to be faithful—to continue steadfastly and attentively in prayer that is rooted in the soil of thanksgiving. In what ways do the following verses reinforce Paul's directive to be devoted in prayer?

- Romans 8:26-27
- Philippians 4:6
- 1 Thessalonians 5:17-18

LEARNING TO LIVE FAITHFULLY

In our desire to keep in step with the Spirit and obey his promptings, we should be aware of the Spirit's work in our prayer lives, which we see in Romans 8:26-27. E. M. Bounds described the Spirit's ministry in this way:

> He pleads for us and in us. He quickens, illumines, and inspires our prayers. He proclaims and elevates the matter of our prayers, and inspires the words and feelings of our prayers. He works mightily in us so that we can pray mightily. He enables us to pray always and ever according to the will of God.[101]

What comfort and consolation to know that in our weaknesses, we have the assurance of the Spirit's presence presiding over our prayers. The knowledge of the Holy Spirit's assistance enables us to freely and confidently be devoted to prayer.

One of the ways the Holy Spirit enables us to pray according to the will of God is through Scripture. S. D. Gordon wrote, "Bible reading is the listening side of prayer."[102] Certainly if prayer is a conversation between the Lord and me, then when I read his Word with a listening heart, he is speaking to me. This thought has changed how I pray. Since the Word is inspired by God and is profitable for teaching, reproof, correction, and training in righteousness (2 Timothy 3:16), I find I respond to what I have read by praying the Word back to God—not just for myself, but for others also.

We find numerous prayers sprinkled throughout Scripture that we can use as our own. The psalms are ready-made prayers and so often express our thoughts and feelings. Another prayer I like is found in Hebrews 13:21, and I personalize it in this way: "Lord, equip me with all I need for doing your will. Produce in me through the power of Jesus Christ every good thing that is pleasing to you." Another good prayer is Psalm 139:23-24: "Search me, O God, and know my heart; test me and know my anxious thoughts.

Point out anything in me that offends you, and lead me along the path of everlasting life."

Andrew Murray wrote about the intertwined relationship between prayer and Scripture, "As you enter a time of private prayer, let your first focus be to give thanks to God for the unspeakable love that invites you to come to Him and to converse freely with Him. Prepare yourself for prayer by Bible study. . . . Take time to present yourself reverently and in quietness before God."[103]

The faithful way is paved with faithful prayer.

REMAINING FAITHFUL

As we faithfully devote ourselves to prayer, we grow in our conscious dependence on Christ—a dependency that allows us to come to the end of the day and say, "Amen."

- What would you consider to be your greatest hindrance to spending time in prayer?

- In what way have you been encouraged to be faithful in prayer?

Father, I pray that your love will overflow more and more, and that I will keep on growing in knowledge and understanding. For I want to understand what really matters so that I may live a pure and blameless life until the day of Christ's return (see Philippians 1:9-10). Amen.

If we might slip away into a quiet corner, with the old Book open, and the knee bent, and the will bent, until we come to see things through God's eye, and yield ourselves to God's plan. Then we will learn to pray. And nothing shall be held back.

S. D. GORDON, *Five Laws That Govern Prayer*

the fruit of the Spirit

The Holy Spirit produces this kind of fruit in our lives: love, joy, peace, patience, kindness, goodness, faithfulness, gentleness, and self-control.

GALATIANS 5:22-23

Faithfulness is a fruit of the Spirit. Such faithfulness believes God's Word, clings to Him, and waits in perfect trust that His power will accomplish all that He has promised.

ANDREW MURRAY,

God's Word for Growing in Prayer

THE EXTRAORDINARY BY-PRODUCT of abiding in Christ is the fruit we bear. Andrew Murray made this observation about the fruit of abiding:

> If Christ, the heavenly Vine, has taken the believer as a branch, then He has pledged Himself, in the very nature of things, to supply the sap and spirit and nourishment to make it bring forth fruit. . . . The soul need but have one care—to abide closely, fully, wholly. He will give the fruit. He works all that is needed to make the believer a blessing.[104]

The Holy Spirit produces *fruit*, not fruits. The word is singular; all nine fruits are a unified whole. However, while there is balance and symmetry among the traits, most scholars agree that since *love* is mentioned first, it can be considered the principle fruit.

The first three characteristics mentioned in Galatians relate to God:

- *Love* is divine, unconditional love. "The marvelous tender passion—the love of God—heightless, depthless, shoreless, shall flood our hearts, making us as gentle and tender-hearted and self-sacrificing and gracious as He."[105]

- *Joy* springs from God's love and is dependent not on our circumstances but on God's eternal love and acceptance of us. "Life need not be easy to be joyful. Joy is not the absence of trouble but the presence of Christ."[106]

- *Peace* is a gift from the Prince of Peace. "Peace is the deliberate adjustment of my life to the will of God."[107] "For peace of mind, resign as general manager of the universe."[108]

The next three traits relate to interactions with others:

- *Patience* is long-suffering. It is even-tempered under provocation, willing to wait and to endure. "Quiet waiting before God would save from many a mistake and from many a sorrow."[109]

- *Kindness* is thoughtfulness, compassion, and selflessness. I once saw a T-shirt with this recommendation: "In a world where you can be anything—be kind."

- *Goodness* is love in action. "Genuine goodness is a matter of habitually acting and responding appropriately in each situation as it arises, moved always by the desire to please God."[110]

The last three elements are for us:

- *Faithfulness* is dependability, loyalty. Theodore Roosevelt commented, "It is better to be faithful than famous."[111]

- *Gentleness* is merciful, tender, sympathetic. "Let your gentleness be evident to all" (Philippians 4:5, NIV). "It sweetens the temper; corrects an irritable disposition; makes the heart kind; disposes us to make all around us as happy as possible."[112]

- *Self-control* is self-discipline, strength to control our sinful desires. "A person without self-control is like a city with broken-down walls" (Proverbs 25:28). "If you would learn self-mastery, begin by yielding yourself to the One Great Master."[113]

Taken as a whole, the fruit of the Spirit seems to illustrate a life that is lived faithfully—a worthy life filled with love, joy, and peace—a life whose only care is to abide in the Vine.

EXPLORING THE WORD

Warren Wiersbe shared this truth: "We do not bear fruit for our own consumption; we bear fruit that others might be fed and helped, and that Christ might be glorified."[114] How do these Scriptures help you further understand the fruit of the Spirit?

- 1 Corinthians 13:4-7
- Colossians 3:12-15

LEARNING TO LIVE FAITHFULLY

What does someone look like when he or she allows the Holy Spirit to produce fruit? Jim Cymbala, pastor of Brooklyn Tabernacle, relates a touching story about one of his mentors, the late Howard Goss. Many years after Howard's death, Jim met with Howard's son, who shared about his dad:

> My dad really walked with God. As a pastor he
> was quite famous and everybody wanted him
> to speak, especially at those huge summer-camp
> meetings. But all the acclaim and popularity, all
> the invitations and compliments, never affected
> him except to make him more humble before God.
> I'll never forget one big camp meeting when I was
> a kid. Every famous preacher was invited and the
> crowds were tremendous. Meetings were held all
> day long—morning, afternoon, and night—and
> all the visiting preachers jockeyed for positions
> hoping to speak during the night rallies when the
> attendance was the largest.

When they were making the schedule, one of the leaders asked where my father was. No one knew. They finally found him in the kitchen down on his hands and knees scrubbing the floor. When told that the schedule was being made and they wanted to know his preference, he replied, "Oh, brothers, you've got so many good preachers here that you don't need to worry about me. But I found out that they're short of help here in the kitchen so I thought I'd lend a hand." Tears welled up in their eyes as the son reminisced about his father whose godly heart had left such a deep impression on so many.[115]

Although Howard exemplified the fruit of the Spirit, anyone who knew him would probably characterize him as a humble, faithful servant. Faithfulness tends to be a fairly noticeable part of the fruit, so it is all-important to abide closely, fully, and wholly.

REMAINING FAITHFUL

Howard Goss's son remembered his dad as always seeking God. He was a man who was often seen on his knees in his study. We can do many things without abiding in Christ, but bearing fruit will never be one of them.

- Take time to evaluate how each element of the fruit of the Spirit is exhibited in your life.

- In what way do you see faithfulness being produced by the Spirit as you abide in Christ?

Father, it is a privilege to abide and an honor to bear your fruit. May my abiding bless others and bring you glory as I walk the faithful way. Amen.

Fruit grows in a climate blessed with an abundance of the Spirit and the Word. . . . This involves the Word, prayer, worship, praise, and fellowship with God's people. It also means "pulling out the weeds" so that the seed of the Word can take root and bear fruit.

WARREN WIERSBE, *Be Free*

running faithfully

*Since we are surrounded by such a huge crowd
of witnesses to the life of faith, let us strip off
every weight that slows us down, especially the
sin that so easily trips us up. And let us run with
endurance the race God has set before us. We do
this by keeping our eyes on Jesus, the champion
who initiates and perfects our faith.*

HEBREWS 12:1-2

*We are going to run, not because of the prize at
the end and not because so many illustrious saints
have run the course in the past and have been
gloriously crowned, but because the vision of Jesus
thrills the soul.*

JOHN PHILLIPS, *Exploring Hebrews*

When I was visiting with a friend who had just completed her first half marathon, she recounted how it had taken months to be able to run even one mile, but because of her strong desire to accomplish her goal, she succeeded. The discipline and diligence it took were worth the reward of crossing the finish line and receiving hugs and congratulations.

The author of Hebrews illustrated the life of faith as a race, one that is to be run freely and steadfastly. Setting our hearts to run with endurance is all-important as we seek to live faithfully. Lawrence Richards defines *perseverance* this way: "Perseverance is overcoming difficulties: it is facing pressures and trials that call for a steadfast commitment to doing right and maintaining a godly life."[116]

As a young captive in Babylon, Daniel was one of the faithful witnesses who, when faced with trials, was steadfastly committed to doing right. In Daniel 1:8 we learn, "Daniel was determined not to defile himself by eating the food and wine given to them by the king." To follow the Lord's law, Daniel proposed a ten-day special diet—and it was so successful that he and his friends looked healthier and better nourished than the other young men. Consequently he and his friends were exempt from the king's diet. Even in the midst of challenging circumstances, Daniel was determined to run his race faithfully.

EXPLORING THE WORD

Perseverance means steadily advancing because the goal is worth the effort. Such perseverance requires dedication to keep going despite obstacles that could hinder progress. What do you learn in these verses about the importance of perseverance?

- Romans 5:3-5
- Philippians 3:13-14
- James 1:2-4

LEARNING TO LIVE FAITHFULLY

We really do not need to be reminded that we are in a race. Our lives seem to be filled not just with running but also periodic hurdles placed on our paths along the way. The reality is that we are in a spiritual race, one prescribed by God. Let us run on his appointed path with the training manual he has provided.

This race is an age-old race run by a great crowd of faithful witnesses who have gone before us. They have run their course, overcome, and triumphed. *Witness* does not mean spectator. Heroes like Daniel bear witness to the sufficiency of the Lord because he equipped them to run the race faithfully.

Hebrews 12:1 tells us to strip off every weight that slows us down. A weight is anything that can impede our progress. Weights are not necessarily sin; in fact, they are usually legitimate activities that subtly take the edge off of running well. Consider busyness, for example. Oswald Chambers reminds us that "the things that are right, noble, and good from the natural standpoint are the very things that keep us from being God's best."[117]

This passage in Hebrews also compares sin to a piece of clothing that could wind itself around our legs, entangle us, and cause us to trip. We must strip off these entanglements if we want to run our races well. And because of the indwelling presence of the Holy Spirit, we have the power to do so.

Running with endurance means setting your heart to stay faithful for the entire race. The race of faith is not a hundred-yard dash—it is a lifelong journey on the path the Lord has marked out for you. In Isaiah God gives us this promise: "I am the LORD your God, who teaches you what is good for you and leads you along the paths you should follow" (Isaiah 48:17). We know we can persevere because of Christ and the multitudes who have endured before us. As Paul confidently stated, "I can do everything through Christ, who gives me strength" (Philippians 4:13).

We endure by keeping our eyes on Jesus. Warren Wiersbe commented, "*To look* means 'to trust.' . . . Christ is both the exemplar *and the enabler*! As we see Him in the Word and yield to His Spirit, He increases our faith and enables us to run the race."[118] We look to Jesus because he is the champion—the founder and perfecter of our faith who endured the cross for the joy set before him.

In Hebrews 10:35-36 we find this exhortation: "Do not throw away this confident trust in the Lord. Remember the great reward it brings you! Patient endurance is what you need now, so that you will continue to do God's will. Then you will receive all that he has promised." We desire to run faithfully and with perseverance because Jesus is more than worthy to receive our steadfast commitment—for he indeed thrills the soul.

REMAINING FAITHFUL

I read of a race in ancient Greece where what mattered was not winning first place, but crossing the finish line with your torch burning. To finish our race with our torches burning necessitates running intentionally, temptation-aware, and dependent upon the Holy Spirit—all key elements of running faithfully.

- What discipline do you need to consider in order to run with endurance?

- As you examine your life, identify what weights or sins need to be addressed in order to run freely.

Father, may I fix my eyes on you as I run my race, trusting you to strengthen me for the path you have set before me. And Lord, may I keep my torch burning. Amen.

May I run the race before me,
    strong and brave to face the foe,
looking only unto Jesus
    as I onward go.

KATE B. WILKINSON,
"May the Mind of Christ My Savior"

authentic faithfulness

Why do you keep calling me "Lord, Lord!" when
you don't do what I say?

LUKE 6:46

Faith is the heroic effort of your life, you fling
yourself in reckless confidence on God.

OSWALD CHAMBERS,
My Utmost for His Highest

ONE MORNING IN RUSSIA, two soldiers burst into a church service. With rifles in hand, they shouted, "All those who are faithful to God, move to the right side of the church. . . . You will be shot for your faith. You who wish to go home and keep your life, stand on the left side." Stunned and terrified, the congregation slowly separated—those on the left side stood apologetically, and those on the right had "their eyes closed in last-minute prayers." After the people on the left had filed out, the soldiers put down their weapons. "'We, too, are Christians,' they said, 'but we wish to worship without hypocrites.'"[119]

The word *hypocrite* is taken from the Greek word *hupokritēs*, which means "an actor" or a "pretender," a "two-faced person . . . whose profession does not match their practice" or "who 'says one thing but does another.'"[120] But as C. S. Lewis observed, "God is not deceived by externals."[121] An authentic person, one whose words and deeds emerge from a consistent character, is genuine, reliable, and dependable.

Those who are willing to change their allegiance based on the needs of the moment are, essentially, hypocrites. But as followers of Jesus, we make a firm commitment to remain faithful despite circumstances or how others choose to respond. Our character is steadfast and genuine.

EXPLORING THE WORD

Jesus harshly criticized the Pharisees for their hypocrisy: "What sorrow awaits you teachers of religious law and you Pharisees. Hypocrites! . . . Outwardly you look like righteous people, but inwardly your hearts are filled with hypocrisy and lawlessness" (Matthew 23:27-28). What can you learn about authenticity and hypocrisy from Luke 6:43-49?

LEARNING TO LIVE FAITHFULLY

Outwardly, all the people in that Russian church seemed to be righteous and faithful—until they were forced to decide the authenticity of their faith. It is in the face of temptation, distress, and persecution that our true faith is manifested. When we are willing to compromise, we show that we have built the foundations of our houses on shifting sand.

Jesus clearly stated that good fruit, good thoughts, and a life dedicated to being faithful are necessary to standing firm when we encounter the unpredictabilities of life. Why would we not want to exhibit the good fruit of Christian character? Why would we not want to have good hearts? Why would we not want to have lives built on a solid foundation so that as we journey through this challenging, complex world we do not collapse into heaps of ruins?

What we need to keep remembering is that God is for us. With great love he purchased our freedom and adopted us into his family. Oswald Chambers observed, "Shipwreck occurs where there is not that mental poise which comes from being established on the eternal truth that God is holy love."[122] David proclaimed his desire to respond to this eternal truth in Psalm 116:12-14: "What can I offer the LORD for all he has done for me? I will lift up the cup of salvation and praise the LORD's name for saving me. I will keep my promises to the LORD in the presence of all his people." And so we must answer these pivotal questions: Is our God worthy of our living a sacrificial, faithful life? What cost are we willing to pay to live the faithful way?

Listening to the Lord's teaching and following him in obedience is how we live on solid rock. It is how we avoid becoming hypocrites. Having a passionate desire to honor Christ and stand before him unashamed should be our incentive to do as he asks.

Hugh M'Kail's life was built on solid rock, and he was willing to fling himself in reckless abandon on God. He was a brilliant young man, born in the mid-1600s and educated at the University of Edinburgh. Hugh entered the ministry but was expelled from the state church at age twenty after signing the Presbyterian Covenant, which the Scottish crown considered treasonous. Royal troops pursued him for years. Eventually he was caught and sentenced to be hanged. On the day of his execution, he was up at five, waking his companions, quoting Scripture, and encouraging his friends. As he stood on the scaffold, he looked out at the crowd and lifted his voice to sing Psalm 31:

> In You, O Lord, I put my trust;
> Let me never be ashamed;
> Deliver me in Your righteousness.

VERSE 1, NKJV

And thus, at twenty-six years of age, he died as he had lived: for the Lord.[123] M'Kail stood faithfully on the solid rock, flinging himself in reckless confidence on God.

REMAINING FAITHFUL

Warren Wiersbe wrote that "Paul's greatest fear was not of death; it was that he might deny his Lord or do something else that would disgrace God's name."[124] Reflecting on Paul's desire to honor God in all his actions, consider your answers to these questions:

- When you're placed in uncomfortable circumstances where declaring your sincere belief in God would result in ridicule, how do you respond? Why?

- Using Jesus' example of building a firm foundation, describe the ways you are currently building an authentic "house" of faith.

- Prayerfully express your desire to have authentic faith.

Oh Father, thank you for your great love for me. Thank you that I have the privilege of living my life in ways that bring you glory. I do not want to go through life being a pretender. May my faith be authentic, and may I produce good fruit with a good and faithful heart. Amen.

This is the rock to which we must dig down— sacred conviction passing into *real consecration*; the conviction that we owe everything to our God and Saviour, and the determination, in the sight and by the grace of God, to yield our hearts and lives to him. A character thus built . . . will be strong against all assaults. . . . Let the storms come, and it will stand.

W. CLARKSON, IN *The Pulpit Commentary*

hall of faithfulness

This world is not our permanent home; we are looking forward to a home yet to come. Therefore, let us offer through Jesus a continual sacrifice of praise to God, proclaiming our allegiance to his name.

HEBREWS 13:14-15

We may remark, that the life of the patriarchs was, in all essential respects, such as we should lead. They looked forward to heaven; they sought no permanent possessions here; they regarded themselves as strangers and pilgrims on the earth. So should we be.

ALBERT BARNES,
Barnes' Notes on the New Testment

To visit a Christian "Hall of Faithfulness," all you have to do is turn to Hebrews 11 in your Bible. Many in the crowd of witnesses who have run the race before us are mentioned in this chapter. The author of Hebrews highlights numerous lives of Old Testament men and women who were not perfect but demonstrated faith.

Abraham stands out as one of the leading patriarchs who willingly obeyed the Lord. When told to leave his home and travel to another land, Abraham "went without knowing where he was going. And even when he reached the land God promised him, he lived there by faith—for he was like a foreigner, living in tents. And so did Isaac and Jacob, who inherited the same promise. Abraham was confidently looking forward to a city with eternal foundations, a city designed and built by God" (Hebrews 11:8-10). These men considered themselves pilgrims and sojourners, not residents who would need permanent possessions.

Keeping an eternal perspective is a key to living faithfully. Paul urged the church in this way:

Since you have been raised to new life with Christ, set your sights on the realities of heaven, where Christ sits in the place of honor at God's right hand. Think about the things of heaven, not the things of earth. For you died to this life, and your real life is hidden with Christ in God. And when Christ, who is your life, is revealed to the whole world, you will share in all his glory.

COLOSSIANS 3:1-4

Evangelist Vance Havner observed, "If you are a Christian, you are not a citizen of this world trying to get to heaven; you are a citizen of heaven making your way through this world."[125]

The patriarchs paved the way by setting their eyes on the realities of heaven. Knowing that we will see Jesus seated at God's right hand and that we will share in Christ's glory are incredible reasons to travel the faithful way.

EXPLORING THE WORD

Looking forward to our heavenly home is a part of fixing our eyes on Jesus as we run our race. Thinking about things of heaven and not of earth frees us from becoming attached to the world so we can put to death earthly things that weigh us down and trip us up. What encouragement do you receive from these verses?

- John 14:1-3
- 2 Peter 3:10-13

LEARNING TO LIVE FAITHFULLY

Hebrews mentions stalwarts of the faith such as Noah, Moses, and David, but we also read there of others who were tortured, chained in prison, stoned, and even sawed in half. These people, though faced with horrendous trials, "placed their hope in a better life after the resurrection" (Hebrews 11:35).

Today, the Hall of Faithfulness continues to be filled with unsung heroes. After nineteen-year-old Varia came to Christ, she fearlessly went forward at a communist youth organization meeting, gave her testimony, and begged everyone to give up the way of sin and accept Christ. She was immediately arrested and taken to prison. When asked if she regretted what she did, she replied, "No, and if they free me I would do it again. Don't think that I suffer. I am glad that God loves me so much and gives me the joy to endure for his name." The last anyone heard of Varia was in a letter she wrote: "Please pray for me that I may remain faithful until the end. . . . Don't worry about us. We are glad and joyful because our reward in heaven is great!"[126]

What a profound summary of what we should strive for on our journeys: to race toward heaven with a desire to remain joyfully faithful. The knowledge that we have died to this life and that our real lives are hidden with Christ in God gives us boldness and freedom to serve faithfully, trusting the Lord wholeheartedly. Countless brothers and sisters hold fast to their faith because they know the best is yet to come. Whether we remain faithful under persecution or in mundane, obscure circumstances, we do so because we look forward with hope for our home yet to come.

Randy Alcorn, founder and director of Eternal Perspective Ministries, wrote,

> Set your sights on Jesus Christ, the Rock of salvation. He is the one who has promised to prepare a place for those who put their hope in him, a place where they will live with him forever. If we can learn to fix our eyes on Jesus, to see through the fog and picture our eternal home in our mind's eye, it will comfort and energize us, giving us a clear look at the finish line.[127]

Those who enter the Hall of Faithfulness consider themselves to be pilgrims passing through this world. While here, though, they live hopeful, faithful lives because their eyes are fixed on Jesus and their eternal home.

REMAINING FAITHFUL

David had this perspective: "I am your guest—a traveler passing through, as my ancestors were before me" (Psalm

39:12). We are pilgrims—guests running our races to our permanent home. Heaven is our finish line; we want to cross it strong and confident in our devotion as we enter the Hall of Faithfulness, eager to hear, "Well done, my good and faithful servant" (Matthew 25:23).

- In what ways have you been challenged to live the faithful way?

- What can help you keep an eternal perspective and set your sights on the realities of heaven?

Father, thank you for the testimony and sacrifice of your faithful children. I pray that my faithfulness might encourage others. Thank you for the hope I have and the promise of my eternal home. I offer a continual sacrifice of praise and allegiance to your name. Amen.

No eye has seen, no ear has heard,
    and no mind has imagined
what God has prepared
    for those who love him.

I CORINTHIANS 2:9

well done!

His master said to him, "Well done, good and
faithful servant. You have been faithful over a
little; I will set you over much. Enter into the joy
of your master."

MATTHEW 25:21, ESV

God's method is to take account of character, of
motive, of the way in which a person makes use of
what is entrusted to him. Thus they who produce
most results will not be honoured more than those
people whose efforts result in less visible effects, but
who are equally faithful with their smaller gifts.

W. F. ADENEY, IN *The Pulpit Commentary*

In the Parable of the Three Servants, Jesus illustrated the Kingdom of Heaven by telling the story of a master preparing to leave on a long trip. The master gathers his servants and gives them money to invest while he is gone. He portions out the money according to the abilities of each man: To one he gives five bags of silver, to another two bags, and to a third one bag.

Upon returning, the master calls his servants to give an account of how they used his money. The first and second servants approach their master with news that they have doubled his investment. To each of them the master gives the same praise: "Well done, my good and faithful servant. You have been faithful in handling this small amount, so now I will give you many more responsibilities. Let's celebrate together!" The third servant, though, buried his money and earned no return on the money he was given. The master takes away this servant's money and punishes him for his faithlessness (see Matthew 25:14-30).

One commentator wrote, "The original word, *Ev*, well done, has a peculiar force and energy, far beyond what we can express in English. It was used by auditors or spectators in any public exercise, to express the highest applause, when any part had been excellently performed."[128]

The first two servants were praised not for their success, but for their faithfulness to their master. Although there was a disparity in the amount of money given and gained, there was equality in their faithfulness, and the reward was the same.

The third servant was negligent, unfaithful, and unprofitable. Expositor Lukyn Williams observed, "Men endeavor to screen themselves from blame by minimizing their talents, ability, opportunities; this parable unveils the flimsiness of this pretense, shows that all have responsibilities, and are answerable for the use they make of the graces and faculties, be they never so small."[129]

Jesus also taught, "If you are faithful in little things, you will be faithful in large ones" (Luke 16:10). I believe this verse implies that faithfulness is a lifestyle: We are not only faithful in dealing with money but also in our dealings with our families and friends, in the use of our possessions, in serving others, and in sharing the gospel. Whatever we do, we are to do it to the glory of God—and do it faithfully.

We live faithfully because . . .

- God loves us perfectly and is constantly faithful to us. "Love is the greatest thing that God can give us, and it is the greatest we can give God."[130]

- God gave us sufficient grace through sending his Son to die on the cross to regenerate, justify, and sanctify us. "Life for life; He gave His life for us to possess that we might give our life for Him to possess."[131]

- Our sins are forgiven. "The Spirit that now lives inside me is a Warrior Spirit, who by grace does battle with my sin even in moments when I don't care to. His redemptive zeal is unstoppable. Think of Peter, who denied any knowledge of Christ. Was it the end of his story? No, but not because Peter had the sense to pursue Jesus; it was because Jesus, in unrelenting, forgiving grace, pursued Peter."[132]

- The Holy Spirit indwells us, guiding us through his mastery and influence. "Friendship with God means such oneness of spirit with Him that He may do with us and through us what He wills."[133]

- God's discipline strengthens us and permits us to share in his holiness. "Testings by God. Temptings by Satan. . . . God will test for love's sake to strengthen. Satan will tempt for hate's sake to trip us up and weaken. God's testings will give strength for Satan's temptings."[134] "To become 'partakers of God's holiness' is to be educated for spending eternity with God."[135]

- We abide in Christ and bear the fruit of the Spirit. "See you to the abiding; He will see to the fruit, for He will give it in you and through you."[136]

- We throw ourselves in reckless confidence on God, not wanting to do something permanently foolish because we are temporarily tempted. "Every moment of resistance to temptation is a victory."[137]

- There is a prize—a crown of righteousness—awaiting us. "A grander moment for the Christian athlete, when . . . the pierced hands of Jesus place upon his head the crown of glory!"[138]

- We want to meet the Lord with our torch burning and hear "Well done! Excellent!" as we enter into the jubilant joy of the Lord—for "joy is the serious business of heaven."[139]

- We want Paul's testimony to be ours: "I have fought the good fight, I have finished the race, and I have remained faithful" (2 Timothy 4:7).

Let us run our race faithfully and with endurance for the heavenly prize that awaits us (Philippians 3:14). How thrilling to know that as we "press on" in faithfulness we will receive the crown of righteousness and a glorious "Well done!"

I sit a few feet from a man on death row. Jewish by birth. Tentmaker by trade. Apostle by calling. His days are marked. I'm curious about what bolsters this man as he nears his execution. So I ask some questions.

Do you have family, Paul? *I have none.*

What about your health? *My body is beaten and tired. . . .*

Any awards? *Not on earth.*

Then what do you have, Paul? No belongings. No family. . . . What do you have that matters?. . .

I have my faith. It's all I have. But it's all I need. I have kept the faith.[140]

The glorious fight that God gave me I have fought. The course that I was set I have finished, and I have kept the faith. The future for me holds the crown of righteousness which God, the true judge, will give to those who have loved what they have seen of him.

2 TIMOTHY 4:7-8, PHILLIPS

"the Father and the child"

THE FATHER SPOKE:

You have been following the faithful way.

Yes, Father. Choosing to live faithfully places me in
   the center of your will, where I experience your
   presence, protection, and guidance. I've found it is
   the best way.

And what will help you stay your course?

I think I need to be more intentional and aware
   of how important it is to daily yield myself in
   dependence upon the Holy Spirit, who is my ever-
   present help. I do not fight the good fight or run
   my race alone. I can remain faithful.

*Yes, because I love you with an everlasting love, my divine
   power has given you everything to be faithful.*

I am humbled by your faithfulness. I want to be
steadfast because you are steadfast. I want to be
led and strengthened by the power of your Holy
Spirit. I want faithfulness to always be my first
choice. I want to be able to say, "I have remained
faithful."

Blessings, my dear child. Be assured that my love is as vast
as the heavens and my faithfulness reaches beyond the
clouds. I will lead you in the faithful way as you keep
your hand in mine. Your crown awaits you.

suggestions for group study

THE FAITHFUL WAY is a devotional study and can be used for personal devotions or for group study. Sharing insights and lessons learned in a group setting can be a great way to stimulate and encourage each other in your desire to remain steadfast.

The group can decide how often to meet. One suggestion is to have a six-week study where you meet once a week and discuss five daily readings at a time (six for the last week).

Here are some questions to consider for group discussion:

1. As you look back over this week's readings, what spiritual truth stood out to you?

2. In what way can this truth influence your walk of faithfulness?

3. Was there a particular Scripture that taught, reproved, corrected, or trained you in righteousness? Why?

4. What scriptural example impressed you? What lesson can you learn?

5. Were there one or two quotations that encouraged you to live more faithfully?

6. Reflecting on these truths, Scriptures, and biblical examples, do you sense that the Lord is leading you to make a choice or decision that will keep you on the faithful way?

7. Share any prayer requests that relate to your desire to remain steadfast.

notes

1. Dr. Seuss, *Horton Hatches the Egg* (New York: Random House, 1940), n.p.
2. A. C. Hervey, in *Second Timothy*, vol. 21 of *The Pulpit Commentary*, eds. H. D. Spence-Jones and Joseph S. Exell (Peabody, MA: Hendrickson, 1985), 59.
3. Herbert Lockyer, *All the Men of the Bible* (Grand Rapids, MI: Zondervan, 1958), 92.
4. A. W. Tozer, *The Knowledge of the Holy* (New York: Harper & Row, 1961), 9.
5. E. B. Pusey, ed., *Barnes' Notes: The Minor Prophets,* vol. 2 (Grand Rapids, MI: Baker, 1998), 289.
6. Sam Storms, *The Singing God* (Lake Mary, FL: Passio, 2013), 44–45.
7. Pusey, ed., *Barnes' Notes: Minor Prophets*, 289.
8. Dan Kimball, in *Inspired by Tozer*, ed. Lauren Barlow (Ventura, CA: Regal, 2011), 44.
9. Robert J. Morgan, *From This Verse* (Nashville: Thomas Nelson, 1998), July 21.
10. Storms, *Singing God*, 46.
11. *The American Heritage Dictionary of the English Language*, 5th ed. (2016), s.v. "faithfulness."

12. Lawrence O. Richards, *Expository Dictionary of Bible Words* (Grand Rapids, MI: Zondervan, 1985), 259.

13. Joyce Vollmer Brown, *Courageous Christians: Devotional Stories for Family Reading* (Chicago: Moody Press, 2000), 39–41.

14. Warren W. Wiersbe, *The Wiersbe Bible Commentary: New Testament* (Colorado Springs: David C Cook, 2007), 314.

15. Paul David Tripp, *New Morning Mercies: A Daily Gospel Devotional* (Wheaton, IL: Crossway, 2014), January 13.

16. Oswald Chambers, *My Utmost for His Highest,* March 19, https://utmost.org/abraham%E2%80%99s-life-of-faith/.

17. Thomas Obediah Chisholm, "Great Is Thy Faithfulness," in Alan D. Strange and Derrick J. Vander Meulen, eds., *Trinity Psalter Hymnal* (Willow Grace, PA: Joint Venture, 2018), #245.

18. Chambers, *My Utmost for His Highest*, December 27.

19. John Owen, *Overcoming Sin and Temptation,* eds. Kelly M. Kapic and Justin Taylor (Wheaton, IL: Crossway, 2006), 62.

20. Thomas Whitelaw, in *Genesis*, vol. 1 of *Pulpit Commentary,* 48.

21. S. R. Aldridge, in *Romans*, vol. 18 of *Pulpit Commentary*, 175.

22. B. C. Caffin, in *Matthew*, vol. 30 of *Pulpit Commentary*, 374–75.

23. R. Tuck, in *Psalms*, vol. 4 of *Pulpit Commentary,* 151–52.

24. Esther Kerr Rusthoi, "When We See Christ," in *Hymns for the Family of God* (Nashville: Paragon, 1976), #129.

25. John MacArthur, *Slave: The Hidden Truth about Your Identity in Christ* (Nashville: Thomas Nelson, 2010), 16–17.

26. David Roper, *Growing Slowly Wise: Building a Faith That Works* (Grand Rapids, MI: Discovery House, 2000), 112.

27. John Piper, "Why did God Forbid One Tree in Eden?" (sermon), October 18, 2013, Desiring God, https://www.desiringgod.org/interviews/why-did-god-forbid-one-tree-in-eden.

28. George Müller, *The Autobiography of George Müller* (New Kensington, PA: Whitaker House, 1984), 15.

29. Ibid., 16–17.

30. Wiersbe, *Wiersbe Bible Commentary: New Testament*, 593.

31. Donald G. Bloesch, in *The Portable Seminary,* ed. David Horton (Bloomington, MN: Bethany House, 2006), 175.

32. John Piper, "George Mueller's Strategy for Showing God" (sermon), Feb. 3, 2004, Desiring God, https://www.desiringgod .org/messages/george-muellers-strategy-for-showing-god. Used by permission.

33. Richards, *Expository Dictionary of Bible Words*, 122.

34. Ibid., 318–19.

35. Charles R. Swindoll, *The Grace Awakening* (Dallas: Word, 1990), 60.

36. Ibid., 207.

37. William Evans and S. Maxwell Coder, *The Great Doctrines of the Bible* (Chicago: Moody, 1974), 156.

38. Martyn Lloyd-Jones, *God the Holy Spirit* (Wheaton, IL: Crossway, 1997), 172–73.

39. Wayne Grudem, *Systematic Theology* (Grand Rapids, MI: Zondervan, 1994), 746.

40. S. D. Gordon, *Quiet Talks on Power* (New York: Fleming H. Revell, 1903), 45.

41. Brown, *Courageous Christians*, 48.

42. Lawrence O. Richards, *New International Encyclopedia of Bible Words* (Grand Rapids, MI: Zondervan, 2016), 297.

43. Wiersbe, *Wiersbe Bible Commentary: New Testament*, 423–24.

44. Matthew Henry, in Rev. Dr. Leslie F. Church and Gerald W. Peterman, eds., *Zondervan NIV Matthew Henry Commentary: In One Volume* (Grand Rapids, MI: Zondervan, 2010), n.p.

45. Roper, *Growing Slowly Wise*, 65.

46. Warren Wiersbe, *The Wiersbe Bible Commentary: Old Testament* (Colorado Springs: David C Cook, 2007), 443.

47. John Piper, "The War Within: Flesh Versus Spirit" (sermon), June 19, 1983, Desiring God, https://www.desiringgod.org /messages/the-war-within-flesh-versus-spirit.

48. F. W. Adeney, in *Galatians*, vol. 20 of *Pulpit Commentary*, 116.

49. A. W. Tozer, quoted in Bob Kelly, *Worth Repeating: More than 5,000 Classic and Contemporary Quotes* (Grand Rapids, MI: Kregel, 2003), 171.

50. "Joburg Motorists Get Daily Inspiration from Chalkboard

Wisdom!" *SA People News*, September 26, 2016, https://www
.sapeople.com/2016/0926/joburg-motorists-get-daily-inspiration
-chalkboard-wisdom/.

51. Lockyer, *All the Men of the Bible*, 248.

52. Charles Ryrie, *The Ryrie NAS Study Bible* (Chicago, IL: Moody, 1976), footnote, 241.

53. Tripp, *New Morning Mercies*, September 5.

54. W. Clarkson, in *Proverbs*, vol. 9 of *Pulpit Commentary*, 80.

55. Herbert Lockyer, *All the Women of the Bible* (Grand Rapids, MI: Zondervan, 1988), 113–14.

56. Matthew Henry, *An Exposition of the Old and New Testament* (London: J. O. Robinson, 1828), 1280.

57. Albert Barnes, "Hebrews," in *Barnes' Notes on the New Testament*, ed. Robert Free (Grand Rapids, MI: Baker, 1998), 300.

58. R. Winterbotham, in *Numbers*, vol. 2 of *Pulpit Commentary*, 155.

59. Jerry Bridges, *The Discipline of Grace* (Colorado Springs: NavPress, 1994), 90.

60. Evans and Coder, *Great Doctrines of the Bible*, 292.

61. Ibid., 292.

62. Chambers, *My Utmost for His Highest*, April 6.

63. Jerry Bridges, *Transforming Grace* (Colorado Springs: NavPress, 2017), 32.

64. Paraphrase of the following text from Stevenson's essay entitled "Old Mortality": "that game of consequences to which we all sit down," in *Memories and Portraits* (New York: Charles Scribner's Sons, 1985), 42.

65. Thomas Brooks, *Precious Remedies against Satan's Devices* (Carlisle, PA: Banner of Truth, 1968), 45.

66. W. F. Adeney, in *Proverbs*, vol. 9 of *Pulpit Commentary*, 70.

67. Vince Lombardi, quoted in *Never Scratch a Tiger with a Short Stick*, comp. Gordon S. Jackson (Colorado Springs: NavPress, 2003), 147.

68. J. R. Thomson, in *Mark*, vol. 2 of *Pulpit Commentary*, 249.

69. E. Bickersteth, in *Mark*, vol. 2 of *Pulpit Commentary*, 235.

70. Chambers, *My Utmost for His Highest,* April 15.

71. Phil Ryken, *When Trouble Comes* (Wheaton, IL: Crossway, 2016), 71.

72. Billy Sunday, quoted in Kelly, *Worth Repeating*, 314.

73. William Osler, quoted in Kelly, *Worth Repeating*, 314.

74. Lockyer, *All the Men of the Bible*, 320.

75. Oswald Chambers, *The Quotable Oswald Chambers*, comp. and ed. David McCasland (Grand Rapids, MI: Discovery House, 2008), 258.

76. Donald G. Bloesch, in *Portable Seminary*, 175.

77. Ibid., 167.

78. Thomas Carlyle, quoted in Martin H. Manser, comp., *The Westminster Collection of Christian Quotations* (Louisville, KY: Westminster John Knox, 2001), 345.

79. Lockyer, *All the Men of the Bible*, 336.

80. Robert Sanderson, quoted in "Psalm 19," Charles Spurgeon, *Treasury of David*, 296.

81. Brother Andrew with John and Elizabeth Sherrill, *God's Smuggler* (Minneapolis: Chosen, 2015), 37–38.

82. E. Hurndall, in *First Corinthians*, vol. 19 of *Pulpit Commentary*, 348.

83. Brooks, *Precious Remedies against Satan's Devices*, 67.

84. Erwin W. Lutzer, quoted in *Westminster Collection of Christian Quotations*, 372.

85. John Willison, "Psalm 119," in *Treasury of David*, vol. 3, 268.

86. Gary Inrig, *Quality Friendship* (Chicago: Moody, 1981), 55.

87. Quoted by E. Johnson in *Proverbs*, vol. 9 of *Pulpit Commentary*, 525.

88. Lloyd-Jones, *God the Holy Spirit*, 228.

89. C. Lipscomb, in *First Corinthians*, vol. 19 of *Pulpit Commentary*, 298.

90. Barnes, "Romans," in *Barnes' Notes on the New Testament*, 263–64.

91. Finlayson, in *Philippians*, vol. 20 of *Pulpit Commentary*, 69.

92. Evans, *Great Doctrines of the Bible*, 116.

93. Wiersbe, *Wiersbe Bible Commentary: New Testament*, 615.

94. F. W. Faber, in Mary Wilder Tileston, *Joy and Strength for the Pilgrim's Day* (Boston: Little, Brown, 1901), April 21.

95. Gordon, *Quiet Talks on Power*, 193.

96. Erwin W. Lutzer, quoted in *Westminster Collection of Christian Quotations*, 172.

97. R. A. Torrey, *How to Pray* (Chicago: Moody, n.d.), 59.

98. Gordon, *Quiet Talks on Power*, 168.

99. Voice of the Martyrs, *Extreme Devotion* (Nashville: W, 2001), 188.

100. Martin Smith, *The Word Is Very Near You* (Lanham, MD: Cowley, 1989), 20.

101. E. M. Bounds, *The Complete Works of E. M. Bounds on Prayer: Book Four, The Reality of Prayer* (Grand Rapids, MI: Baker, 1990), 57.

102. S. D. Gordon, *Five Laws That Govern Prayer* (Chicago: Revell, 1925), 13.

103. Andrew Murray, *Power in Prayer* (Minneapolis: Bethany House, 2011), 60.

104. Andrew Murray, *Abide in Christ* (Springdale, PA: Whitaker House, 1979), 130.

105. Gordon, *Quiet Talks on Power*, 180.

106. William Vander Hoven, quoted in *Westminster Collection of Christian Quotations*, 214.

107. Anonymous, quoted in Kelly, *Worth Repeating*, 262.

108. Larry Eisenberg, quoted in Kelly, *Worth Repeating*, 261.

109. James Hudson Taylor, quoted in *Quotes for the Journey, Wisdom for the Way,* comp. Gordon S. Jackson (Colorado Springs: NavPress, 2000), 174.

110. *The Cloud of Unknowing,* quoted in *Westminster Collection of Christian Quotations*, 147.

111. Theodore Roosevelt, quoted in *Westminster Collection of Christian Quotations*, 103.

112. Barnes, "Galatians," in *Barnes' Notes on the New Testament,* 387.

113. Johann Friedrich Lobstein, quoted in *Westminster Collection of Christian Quotations*, 334.

114. Wiersbe, *Wiersbe Bible Commentary: New Testament,* 576.

115. Adapted from Jim Cymbala with Stephen Sorenson, *The Life God Blesses* (Grand Rapids, MI: Zondervan, 2001), 85–86.

116. Richards, *Expository Dictionary of Bible Words*, 484.

117. Chambers, *My Utmost for His Highest*, December 9.

118. Wiersbe, *Wiersbe Bible Commentary: New Testament*, 839.

119. Voice of the Martyrs, *Extreme Devotion*, 46.

120. BibleHub, s.v. "5273. hupokritēs," accessed April 29, 2019, https://biblehub.com/greek/5273.htm.

121. C. S. Lewis, quoted in *Westminster Collection of Christian Quotations*, 185.

122. Chambers, *My Utmost for His Highest*, May 8.

123. Morgan, *From This Verse*, March 3.

124. Wiersbe, *Wiersbe Bible Commentary: New Testament*, 785.

125. Vance Havner, quoted in *Westminster Collection of Christian Quotations*, 165.

126. Voice of the Martyrs, *Extreme Devotion*, 58–59, 61.

127. Randy Alcorn, *50 Days of Heaven* (Carol Stream, IL: Tyndale, 2006), 4.

128. Doddrige, in "Benson's Commentary," *Bible Hub*, accessed April 12, 2018, https://biblehub.com/commentaries/matthew/25-21.htm.

129. A. Lukyn Williams, in *Matthew*, vol. 15 of *Pulpit Commentary*, 480.

130. Jeremy Taylor, quoted in Kelly, *Worth Repeating*, 145.

131. Andrew Murray, *The True Vine* (Chicago: Moody, n.d.), 107.

132. Tripp, *New Morning Mercies*, December 20.

133. Gordon, *Quiet Talks on Power*, 214.

134. Ibid., 212.

135. C. Jordan, in *Hebrews*, vol. 21 of *Pulpit Commentary*, 366.

136. Murray, *True Vine*, 52.

137. Frederick William Faber, in *Westminster Collection of Quotations*, 372.

138. H. Bremner, in *First Corinthians*, vol. 19 of *Pulpit Commentary*, 311.

139. C. S. Lewis, in *Westminster Collection of Quotations*, 214.

140. Max Lucado, *When God Whispers Your Name* (Nashville: Thomas Nelson, 1999), 94–95.

about the author

Cynthia Heald is a Bible teacher and the author of the popular **Becoming a Woman of . . .** Bible study series. She speaks frequently at national and international women's retreats and seminars. Cynthia and her husband, Jack, serve with The Navigators and live in Tucson, Arizona.

a word about the cover

IN CREATING THE COVER DESIGN, I chose to use imagery of an abstract path, which also looks like the building blocks of life. Little by little, day by day, we choose to stay on that path as we follow Jesus. The path is made up of rich and organic colors to symbolize the richness of our lives in Christ. It is also made up of a variety of sizes of rectangles to reflect the fact that not every day looks the same.

The abstract art also resembles pieces of a quilt being sewn together, as well as stones of remembrance being piled up as a reminder of the path taken. The warm, cream background is antiqued and weathered to show the well-trodden way.

The book and chapter titles were handwritten to communicate that faith is a personal journey. They were created in a humble and quiet cursive style, as opposed to fancy and elegant, to show the reality of life.

JULIE CHEN, SENIOR DESIGNER